PIT BOSS SMOKER COOKBOOK

FOR BEGINNERS

THE COMPLETE GUIDE TO EFFORTLESS GRILLING AND SMOKING WITH EASY-TO-FOLLOW RECIPES, PELLET PAIRING TIPS, AND TIME-SAVING TECHNIQUES FOR FLAWLESS BBQ EVERY TIME

Jack Lawson

SPECIAL BONUSES INSIDE

for organizing the BBQ party of your dreams!

SCAN THE QR CODE
AT THE END OF THE BOOK
AND
GET YOUR BONUSES *NOW!*

THANK YOU FOR PURCHASING MY BOOK!
IF YOU ENJOYED IT, I WOULD APPRECIATE YOUR HONEST FEEDBACK ON AMAZON

If you have any concerns, please email me at:

info@topqualitybooks.com

I want to create high-quality products that give everyone satisfaction

TABLE OF CONTENTS

TABLE OF CONTENTS

Welcome to the world of grilling and smoking excellence! Whether you're an experienced backyard BBQ enthusiast or just starting, this guide is designed to help you master your Pit Boss Smoker. More than just a collection of recipes, it's a complete toolkit to revolutionize your cooking and impress your friends and family at every get-together.

The Pit Boss Smoker stands out for its versatility, power, and ability to deliver restaurant-quality BBQ right in your backyard. Whether smoking brisket, grilling steaks, or trying out seafood, the Pit Boss makes the process enjoyable and easy. But, like any great tool, true mastery comes from understanding its capabilities and learning how to use them to your advantage.

This book will take you from the basics of operating and maintaining your smoker to advanced techniques that will take your BBQ game to the next level.

Your journey with Pit Boss is about to begin. Here's what's in store for you:

- **Getting to Know Your Pit Boss**: We'll start by covering the essentials of the Pit Boss smoker—how it works, its components, and the best practices for maintaining it. With step-by-step instructions, you'll learn how to get the most out of your smoker, from firing it up for the first time to choosing the suitable pellets for every dish.
- **Mastering the Basics**: This section delves into temperature control, smoke management, and critical techniques like direct and indirect grilling. Practical tips will help you manage these elements without hours of trial and error.
- **Quick Start Guide for Beginners**: Only some have the luxury of time to spend hours learning through trial and error. We've included a quick start guide to get you going immediately. The goal is to give you the confidence to light up your Pit Boss and start smoking your first meal without the usual stress and uncertainty.

- **Pellets and Flavor Pairings:** A central question for most BBQ enthusiasts is: Which pellets work best with what meats? This book offers a dedicated section to help you pair different wood pellets with various types of meat, ensuring that your meals always hit the right flavor notes—no more guesswork—just results that will leave everyone asking for seconds.
- **Troubleshooting Common Issues:** Even the most experienced pitmasters face challenges, and the last thing you want is to be caught off guard during a big family BBQ. This book offers a detailed troubleshooting guide to help you overcome common issues, like fluctuating temperatures, meat that's too dry, or overwhelming smoke flavors.
- **Succulent recipes to get you started:** Dive into a collection of meticulously curated recipes designed for your Pit Boss. There's something for every palate and occasion: luscious meats to flavorful fish and seafood, from vibrant vegan and vegetarian options to delicious desserts and snacks. These recipes are designed for real life: minimal prep time, straightforward instructions, and guaranteed results that impress even the harshest critics.
- **Advanced Pit Boss Techniques:** For those ready to take their grilling to the next level, we explore advanced techniques such as mixing pellets to achieve custom flavors.

Grilling is more than just cooking; it is an art that brings people together, creating memories that last a lifetime. As you flip through the pages, we encourage you to experiment, learn, and, most importantly, enjoy every moment behind the grill. By the end of this book, you'll feel confident in your Pit Boss Smoker and have a collection of go-to recipes and techniques you can rely on for any occasion.

So fire up your Pit Boss, grab your favorite pellets, and start the journey to BBQ mastery!

WELCOME TO THE PIT BOSS FAMILY

GET FAMILIAR WITH YOUR PIT BOSS

In today's age, as people increasingly seek culinary adventures and outdoor cooking experiences, the Pit Boss Wood Pellet Grill and Smoker have emerged as a groundbreaking alternative to traditional barbecue grills. This innovative cooking apparatus combines the authentic flavors of wood-fired cooking with the precision and convenience of modern technology. Unlike its gas or charcoal counterparts, the Pit Boss uses wood pellets, providing a greener and more flavorful cooking experience without the risk of flare-ups that can spoil the cooking process.

The Pit Boss Wood Pellet Grill and Smoker is the ultimate outdoor cooking appliance, offering exceptional versatility. It operates on compressed sawdust wood pellets, providing an eco-friendly cooking option. Additionally, it offers a distinctive smoking experience, imparting a rich, smoky flavor to a wide variety of foods, including robust meats like pork butt and brisket, delicate fish, vegetables, and even desserts. The grill's ability to maintain low temperatures, around 250 degrees Fahrenheit, ensures that every dish is cooked evenly and infused with the desired smoky taste.

One of the unique features of pellet smokers and grills, including the Pit Boss, is their use of a water pan. This component slows the burning process, absorbing heat to allow food to cook thoroughly without drying out. This method is reminiscent of traditional smoking techniques, where liquids, like beer, are added to enhance flavor and moisture. Incorporating a water pan ensures that the temperature remains consistent, even during extended cooking sessions, providing tender results without the risk of scorching or drying the food.

The Pit Boss grill is designed for efficient cooking. Its internal thermostat maintains a consistent temperature, allowing you to cook your food exactly as you want. The grill also has a grease management system that helps to keep the cooking surface clean and safe. It features a hinged grate that makes it easy to dispose of excess grease, reducing the risk of flare-ups and making the cleaning process a breeze.

The Pit Boss grill is known for its exceptional performance and energy efficiency. It consumes less energy than traditional grills. Its versatile design allows it to use multiple fuel types, giving you more flexibility in how and where you use it. Whether you have a suburban terrace or a spacious backyard, the Pit Boss grill can meet your cooking needs. Some models even come equipped with wheels, making moving and setting up easy.

Durable and designed to withstand the elements, the Pit Boss is constructed from materials like stainless steel, ceramic, or quartz, which resist rust and ensure longevity. When selecting a Pit Boss, consider the size and features that best suit your space and cooking preferences, including options for precise temperature control and storage for wood pellets.

For all the above, The Pit Boss Wood Pellet Grill and Smoker redefine the outdoor cooking landscape by offering a sustainable, versatile, and user-friendly option for enthusiasts and professionals alike. With its ability to grill, smoke, bake, and roast, the Pit Boss invites you to explore an endless array of culinary possibilities while enjoying the unmatched flavor of wood-fired cooking. In this guide, you'll uncover the intricacies of operating your Pit Boss, selecting the perfect wood pellets, and mastering the art of grilling to ensure every meal is memorable.

Mastering a wood pellet smoker or grill might feel daunting at first. However, the Pit Boss simplifies outdoor cooking with its user-friendly design, making it as straightforward as operating a commercial kitchen oven. With the capacity to smoke, grill, bake, roast, and barbecue various foods, from succulent ribs to crispy pizzas and juicy burgers, this appliance is a walk in the park. The Pit Boss functions much like an oven but with a twist that infuses the genuine smokiness and flavor of wood-fired cooking. Here's how:

Pellet Feeding and Ignition: The Pit Boss grill uses wood pellets, which are small cylindrical pieces of wood made from compressed sawdust. These pellets are available in various flavors, such as hickory, mesquite, and applewood. When the grill is activated, an electric igniter ignites the pellets, creating a steady heat and smoke that imparts a unique and flavorful taste to the food. This cooking method cannot be replicated by conventional gas or charcoal grills, resulting in a distinct and delicious flavor profile for your grilled dishes.

Heat and Smoke Distribution: The Pit Boss grill utilizes a cylindrical chamber design to generate indirect heat through the combustion of wood pellets. This innovative approach guarantees that food is cooked uniformly at lower temperatures, safeguarding the natural juices and preventing the outer layers from charring before the inside reaches the ideal level of doneness. In contrast to conventional stovetops that rely on charcoal briquettes for direct heat, the Pit Boss grill provides consistent heat and smoke dispersion for an enhanced cooking experience.

Temperature Control: The Pit Boss grill's performanc hinges on consistently maintaining precise temperatures Whether slow smoking at low temperatures for prolonged periods or high-heat searing, the grill's internal thermosta and digital control panel allow accurate adjustments. Th vents and dampers work in tandem to finely regulate airflow, ensuring even temperature distribution throughou cooking. This is akin to the heat control in a convectior oven, which quickly sears meat while retaining its natura juices. This level of temperature control ensure. exceptional cooking results every time, whether you're slow-cooking a brisket or achieving the perfect sear on a steak.

Convection Mechanism: The Pit Boss grill employs ar advanced convection system to produce outstanding cooking outcomes. The auger delivers the pellets for burning and consistently expels hot air, resulting in a steady flame, even at lower temperatures. This design minimizes flare-ups, ensuring that the food is uniformly cooked and achieves an even coloration throughout. The Pit Boss is specifically crafted to facilitate a convection mechanism.

Eco-Friendly and Efficient Fuel: Wood pellets are a superior fuel option because they are more sustainable and efficient than traditional fuels. When used in a closed system, they burn hotter and cleaner, optimizing fuel usage and reducing emissions. Most wood pellets are made from waste wood, promoting a circular economy and supporting a cleaner, sustainable future. By using wood pellets with the Pit Boss, you not only enhance your cooking experience but also contribute to environmental conservation.

Electricity-Powered Functionality: The Pit Boss operates on electricity, blending modern convenience with traditional cooking methods. The grill's electrical components, including the igniter and fan, make outdoor cooking easy and user-friendly.

The Pit Boss redefines outdoor cooking with its precision, versatility, and flavor. It combines the rustic appeal of wood-fired cuisine with the convenience of modern culinary techniques. Understanding how this grill works is essential to unlocking its full potential and exploring various recipes and methods.

Let's explore the incredible features and components that make the Pit Boss Wood Pellet Grill and Smoker a versatile tool in your outdoor cooking arsenal. This impressive machine is more than just a grill—it's a gateway to creating dishes packed with flavor, texture, and an undeniable smoky essence that transforms simple ingredients into culinary wonders. To truly appreciate how it all comes together, let's break down each part of the Pit Boss and understand its role in helping you master your grilling and smoking game.

The Cooking Chamber: Where the Magic Happens

The cooking chamber is crucial to every high-quality grill, including the Pit Boss. It's where your food transforms into delicious meals. Made of durable welded steel, the chamber is built to withstand high heat and effectively retain it. While the shape and size of the chamber may differ across models, its main purpose remains consistent —ensuring even heat distribution for perfectly cooked food.

The choice of construction materials is vital. You might encounter chambers with options like solid, ceramic, or ceramic-coated steel plates. These variations offer distinct advantages. For instance, ceramic plates retain heat and maintain consistent cooking temperatures, resulting in fewer fluctuations during cooking. Moreover, ceramic coatings can make cleaning easier, mainly when dealing with harsh, greasy residues from smoking meats or grilling fatty cuts. The multiple exhaust vents also play a critical role in maintaining a balanced temperature inside the chamber. Proper ventilation ensures that smoke circulates evenly, preventing hot spots and creating a uniform cooking environment.

The Auger: Fueling the Fire

The drill plays a crucial role in the Pit Boss, quietly ensuring the system's smooth operation. This small yet powerful component transfers wood pellets from the hopper to the fire pot, acting as the fuel delivery system. It directly influences the temperature inside the cooking chamber by controlling the rate at which the pellets are fed into the fire.

Despite its importance, the drill often goes unnoticed until it malfunctions. A high-quality auger, securely housed in a sealed compartment, guarantees a consistent pellet flow, preventing potential clogs or disruptions. Proper maintenance is critical. Keeping the drill clean and in optimal condition is essential, as any blockage can significantly impact the cooking process, resulting in uneven heat distribution or, worse, a fire going out during cooking.

The Hopper: Your Pellet Storage Solution

The hopper determines how long you can cook without adding more fuel. It's where you load the wood pellets; its size will dictate how long the grill can run without requiring attention. Larger hoppers are particularly beneficial for extended smoking sessions, such as when you're slow-cooking a brisket or pork shoulder and don't want to keep interrupting the process to refill. On most Pit Boss models, the hopper is conveniently located on the side of the grill for easy access, allowing you to refill it as needed without disrupting the cooking. The great thing about the Pit Boss is its automatic pellet feed system, so you don't have to stay by the grill and manually adjust the fuel—set the temperature, and the system will take care of the rest by feeding pellets at the precise rate required to maintain your desired cooking temperature.

The Heating Element: Bringing the Heat

Cooking on a Pit Boss requires precision, starting with the heating element. Instead of using direct combustion like traditional grills, the Pit Boss utilizes a firebox to create heat in a controlled environment. It ignites wood pellets, producing convection airflow that evenly circulates heat throughout the cooking chamber.

This indirect heat makes the Pit Boss ideal for various cooking techniques, from grilling to smoking. It's beneficial for low-and-slow cooking methods, as the consistent and gentle heat prevents food from burning or drying out. Whether searing a steak at high temperatures or slowly smoking ribs over several hours, the heating element and convection system work harmoniously, giving you complete control over your cooking process.

The Control Panel: Precision at Your Fingertips

The Pit Boss is distinguished by its user-friendly control panel, which serves as the grill's central command center. With just the push of a button, you can effortlessly set and monitor the temperature. Whether you're a grilling beginner or an experienced pitmaster, this panel simplifies achieving the perfect cook.

You can finely adjust the temperature, monitor internal meat temperatures (some models have built-in probes), and select cooking modes based on your dish. The control panel also manages safety features, including automatic shutdown in case of overheating, allowing you to cook confidently without constantly watching over the grill. For those who enjoy experimenting, the panel lets you personalize settings according to your preferences, follow recipes precisely, or adjust them to suit your taste.

Now that we've established the essential components let's explore how Pit Boss can elevate your outdoor cooking experience.

Grill-Searing: Locking in Juices and Flavor

Mastering the art of grilling involves perfectly searing meats to create a flavorful crust that locks in juices. The Pit Boss makes searing effortless with its high heat capabilities. Adjusting the pellet feed rate lets you quickly bring the cooking surface to the ideal searing temperature. This allows you to promptly caramelize the exterior of steaks, chops, or vegetables while keeping the inside tender and moist.

The key to achieving a flawless sear is to preheat the grill to a high temperature and ensure that the meat comes into direct contact with the hot grill grates. With the Pit Boss, you can effortlessly reach the perfect searing temperature without worrying about flare-ups or uneven cooking. It's ideal for achieving that restaurant-quality crust right in your backyard.

Smoking: Infusing Depth and Complexity

The Pit Boss excels at smoking. Its ability to maintain consistent low temperatures over long periods makes it perfect for slow-smoking ribs, brisket, and pork shoulder. The real magic of tobacco lies in the wood pellets, which provide heat and infuse your food with rich, smoky flavors

that traditional grills can't match. By controlling the smoke intensity through the drill and pellet feed system, you can tailor the taste of your food to your exact preference. Whether you want a light smoke to gently enhance the flavor of fish or a deep, rich smoke for a hearty beef cut, the Pit Boss makes it easy to achieve. And because it burns pellets cleanly, you don't have to worry about the acrid, bitter taste that can sometimes come from wood chips or charcoal.

Grill-Roasting: Achieving the Perfect Roast

Cooking significant cuts of meat or whole poultry on the Pit Boss is truly an unparalleled experience. The grill's convection system ensures that heat circulates evenly, keeping your roast juicy and succulent without drying it out. The indirect heat creates a delicious crust on the outside while maintaining a tender and flavorful interior.

The Pit Boss's ability to maintain a consistent temperature, especially during long cooking sessions, sets it apart. This reliability is crucial when roasting a turkey or prime rib, as it ensures the meat browns ideally on the outside without burning while reaching the ideal level of doneness inside.

Grill-Sealing: Finishing with a Smoky Touch

Grill-sealing is a method that combines roasting with a final burst of smoke, adding an extra layer of flavor to your dish. This technique works particularly well for foods like pork ribs or chicken, where you want a subtle smoky finish without overpowering the natural flavors. After your meat has cooked through, a brief, intense application of smoke seals in the flavors, resulting in a delicious final product that will surely impress.

Following this Quick Start Guide, you'll be well on your way to mastering your Pit Boss Wood Pellet Grill and smoker. From setting up the grill to maintaining it after each use, these steps ensure that your grill will continue to provide excellent cooking performance for years to come.

Step 1: Unboxing and Setup

The first step to getting started with your Pit Boss Wood Pellet Grill is ensuring it's set up correctly. After unboxing:

- Check that you have all the necessary components as per the instruction manual. The main parts should include the cooking chamber, hopper, auger, fire pot, and control panel.
- Set up the grill on a flat, stable surface, preferably outdoors, in an open area with plenty of ventilation.
- Ensure the grill is positioned away from flammable materials like wooden fences or low-hanging tree branches.

Step 2: Initial Cleaning

Use a damp cloth to wipe down all interior and exterior surfaces to remove any dust or residue from manufacturing or shipping. Clean the cooking grates thoroughly with mild dish soap and warm water, then rinse and dry them. Ensure the hopper and fire pot are clear of debris or packaging materials.

Step 3: Priming the Auger

Preparing the grill is essential to ensure it can smoothly deliver wood pellets. To do this, fill the hopper with your choice of wood pellets. Then, turn on the grill to "Prime" mode or "Feed" setting, depending on the model. This will activate the drill without igniting the pellets, allowing you to fill the auger tube. You can turn off the prime function once the pellets fall into the fire pot.

Step 4: Seasoning the Grill

Before using your Pit Boss grill for the first time, it's crucial to season it. This process requires heating the grill to a high temperature to eliminate residues and establish a protective layer inside the cooking chamber. Start by loading the hopper with pellets and setting the temperature to approximately 350°F. Let the grill operate for 30-45 minutes, keeping the lid closed. This step cleans the grill and enhances its future performance by improving heat retention and flavor.

Step 5: Loading the Hopper with Pellets

Now that your grill is clean and ready, it's time to fill the hopper with enough pellets for your cooking session. The hopper size will determine how long you can cook without refilling. If you're cooking for a short time, half a hopper should do, but for longer smoking sessions, you'll need to fill it up. Always use high-quality wood pellets because low-quality ones can alter the taste of your food and potentially block the auger.

Step 6: Preheating the Grill

Set the grill to the desired cooking temperature, close the lid, and let it preheat for 10-15 minutes. During this time, the grill will ignite the pellets and produce steady, clean smoke from the vents, indicating that it's ready to use.

Step 7: Adjusting the Temperature

Once the Pit Boss is preheated, you can adjust the temperature to match your preferred cooking method. Whether grilling, smoking, or roasting, the Pit Boss allows you to fine-tune the temperature quickly. To sear your food, turn the heat up to 450°F or higher. To smoke, you'll need to lower the temperature to around 200-225°F. The control panel makes it easy to make these adjustments, and the digital readout will show you the current temperature inside the cooking chamber.

Step 8: Cooking

Now it's time to have some fun - cooking! Place your food on the grates, ensuring enough space between items for the smoke to circulate correctly. If your grill has a lid, close it and monitor the internal temperature using the control panel or a meat probe. Remember that the Pit Boss works best with the lid closed, as this helps trap heat and smoke, ensuring even cooking.

Step 9: Monitoring Pellet Levels

Remember to check your pellet levels while cooking. If you're smoking a brisket or cooking for a long time, you might have to top up the hopper with more pellets. The Pit Boss's automatic feed system will take care of the rest, but be sure not to let the hopper go empty, as this could lead to a drop in temperature and disrupt your cooking.

Step 10: Shutting Down the Grill

Once you're done cooking, shutting down your pit boss properly is essential. Set the temperature to its lowest setting or to "Shut Down" mode if your model has it. Let the grill run for 10-15 minutes to ensure any remaining pellets in the fire pot burn off completely. This prevents any leftover fuel from causing issues during your next cook. Afterward, turn the grill off using the power button and let it cool down with the lid open.

Step 11: Cleaning After Cooking

Once the grill has cooled down, it's time to tidy up. Begin by removing the ash from the fire pot using an ash tool or a small shop vacuum. Don't forget to inspect the cooking grates for any leftover food or grease. Use a grill brush to remove the residue, then wipe the grates with a damp cloth. You should spray the grates with a high-temperature grill before cooking for easier cleaning. Also, check the drip tray and grease bucket and empty them as needed to prevent buildup.

Step 12: Regular Maintenance

Remember to take good care of your Pit Boss to ensure it lasts long and performs at its best. Clean out the fire pot every few uses to prevent ash from building up, and regularly check the auger and hopper for any pellet debris that could cause clogs. Remember to inspect the grease management system, ensuring the drip tray is clean, and the grease bucket is emptied regularly. It's also a good idea to wipe the grill's exterior down to prevent rust, especially if it's exposed to the elements.

Step 13: Storing Your Pit Boss

If you don't plan on using your grill for a while, it's essential to store it properly to prevent damage. Start by thoroughly cleaning the grill and removing all ash and grease. Store the grill in a covered area, such as a garage or shed, to shield it from the elements. If outdoor storage is the only option, get a high-quality grill cover to remove moisture, dust, and debris. Also, remember to disconnect and safely store the power cord.

Step 14: Troubleshooting Tips

If the temperature drops or the grill fails to ignite, check the pellet levels and ensure the auger feeds pellets into the fire pot. Excessive smoke might mean there's a pellet jam or low-quality pellets. In such cases, turn off the grill, clean the fire pot, and restart. If the grill still doesn't light, check the igniter to ensure it's working correctly. Remember to refer to your Pit Boss manual regularly for help with everyday issues.

QUICK START GUIDE SCHEME

1. Unboxing and Setup
2. Initial Cleaning
3. Priming the Auger
4. Seasoning the Grill
5. Loading the Hopper with Pellets
6. Preheating the Grill
7. Adjusting the Temperature
8. Cooking
9. Monitoring Pellet Levels
10. Shutting Down the Grill
11. Cleaning After Cooking
12. Regular Maintenance
13. Storing Your Pit Boss
14. Troubleshooting Tips

PELLETS: TYPES AND FLAVORS

Wood pellets are the heart and soul of pellet grilling, providing the heat you need to cook your food and the rich, smoky flavors that make grilling unique. These small but powerful fuel sources are made from compressed sawdust and come in various wood types, each offering its unique flavor profile that can transform your food.

Why Use Wood Pellets

Many grill enthusiasts favor wood pellets for their efficiency. They generate a remarkable amount of heat for the fuel used and retain heat well over time, making them a cost-effective choice for those who want to maximize their cooking without constantly refueling. Additionally, they produce less ash, resulting in easier cleanup. However, while wood pellets are known for burning cleaners, they may not always impart the same intense smoky flavor or texture as natural wood logs.

Types of Wood Pellets

Wood pellets are an excellent way to add delicious flavors to your grilled dishes. There are two main types of wood pellets: **hardwood** and **softwood**. Each type has unique characteristics, offering different flavors and intensities that can enhance various dishes.

Hardwood pellets, such as oak, hickory, and mesquite, are renowned for their bold and robust flavors. They're perfect for meats that can handle more pungent tastes, like beef or game. However, using hardwood pellets carefully is crucial, as over-smoking can result in bitterness.

On the other hand, softwoods like alder and maple offer more subtle and gentle flavors, making them ideal for delicate foods like chicken and fish. They produce less smoke, perfect for infusing flavor without overwhelming the dish.

Many grilling enthusiasts enjoy using a combination of hardwoods and softwoods. These blended pellets offer a balance of robust and subtle flavors, providing greater versatility in your cooking. Whether you're grilling, smoking, or barbecuing, choosing the suitable wood pellets can take the taste of your dishes to the next level.

How to Choose the Right Wood Pellets

Selecting the best wood pellets for your grill and recipe isn't just about picking a random bag off the shelf. There are a few factors to consider to ensure you're getting the most out of your grilling experience:

- **Quality Matters**: Always look for 100% natural wood pellets without fillers or additives. These will give your food a cleaner burn and a more authentic flavor.
- **Match the flavor to the Food**: Different wood types pair better with certain foods. For example, stronger woods like hickory or mesquite are excellent for beef, while fruitwoods like apple or cherry bring out the best

1. in poultry and pork.
- **Pellet Size and Weight**: Believe it or not, the size and weight of the pellets can impact how efficiently they burn. Heavier pellets might burn less cleanly, which could affect the flavor and efficiency of your cooking, especially in a pellet smoker where fuel management is critical.

Wood Pellet Flavors and Their Best Uses

Understanding the unique flavor profiles of different wood pellets can take your grilling to the next level. Here's a quick guide to some of the most popular wood pellet flavors and how to use them:

- **Apple and Cherry**: These sweet and mild fruitwoods make them perfect for lighter meats like pork and poultry. They add a gentle smoke that enhances without overpowering.
- **Alder**: This option is excellent for delicate meats like chicken or fish. It has a neutral, sweet flavor that won't dominate the dish.
- **Hickory**: A classic in the barbecue world, hickory offers a robust and smoky flavor. It's fantastic for bold meats like ribs or brisket but can be mixed with lighter wood to soften its intensity.
- **Maple**: Known for its subtle sweetness, maple is an excellent choice for turkey and pork. It adds a mild, sweet flavor that complements the meat's natural flavors.
- **Mesquite**: If you're after a bold, spicy kick, mesquite is the way to go. Its strong, intense flavor works well with robust meats like beef, but it's not for the faint of heart.
- **Oak**: A versatile option, oak balances apple's lightness and hickory's intensity. It's great for fish, vegetables, and other foods that need a moderate flavor profile.
- **Pecan**: This is a favorite among many grillers. It offers a flavor similar to hickory but a softer, slightly nutty undertone. It's excellent for beef and chicken and works well for many dishes.

The wood pellets you choose can significantly impact the flavor of your food when grilling with a Pit Boss. Don't be afraid to experiment with different types and blends to find what works best for you. Whether you prefer the boldness of hardwoods or the subtlety of softwoods, there's a perfect pellet out there waiting to elevate your next meal.

LEARN TO MASTER YOUR PIT BOSS

MUST-HAVE GRILL ACCESSORIES

Mastering your Pit Boss Wood Pellet Grill and Smoker is more than just learning the ins and outs of grilling and smoking—it's about leveraging the right tools and accessories to enhance your cooking experience and get the most out of every meal. Whether it's about improving convenience, precision, or safety, each accessory makes your time at the grill more efficient and enjoyable while ensuring your dishes come out tasting incredible.

Grate Holder: A Must-Have for Better Control

Sometimes, the most straightforward tools make the most significant difference. The grate holder is one of those essential accessories, but it quickly proves its worth. It lets you switch grates easily without worrying about your food falling through gaps or shifting awkwardly. It's not just a matter of convenience—this tool ensures your food stays exactly where it should be, helping to maintain even cooking and, ultimately, better results.

Grease Trap: Keeping Things Clean and Flavorful

It's crucial to manage grease properly to keep your grill in top condition and ensure delicious food. A well-sized grease trap, capable of holding up to 70 gallons, is essential for capturing excess fat and preventing it from clogging your grill and affecting the flavor of your meals. Investing in a suitable grease trap reduces mess and guarantees that each dish retains clean, pure flavors without being overpowered by burnt grease.

Digital Thermometer: Precision is Key

When it comes to grilling and smoking, precision is non-negotiable. That's where a good digital thermometer comes in. It allows you to closely monitor the internal temperature of your food, helping you ensure that it's cooked to perfection and safe to eat. Whether you're grilling a steak to medium-rare or smoking a brisket low and slow, this tool takes the guesswork out of the process, helping you hit the perfect doneness every time.

Tongs and Fork Set: More Than Just Tools

Tongs and a sturdy fork seem essential, but they are critical in handling your food on the grill. A high-quality set lets you quickly flip, move, and adjust your food, ensuring every piece is cooked evenly and handled carefully. They're not just about function—using the right tools can also help you present your food better, giving it that final touch of professional quality.

Probe Meat Thermometer: Elevating Your Cooking

If your grill still needs to come with built-in probe thermometers, investing in one or two is a smart move, especially when smoking meat. Being able to check the internal temperature of your meats without opening the grill lid means you keep the heat in while still ensuring your food is perfectly cooked. This level of precision brings your cooking to a whole new level, turning the science of grilling into an art.

Side Tables and Storage Box: Organization is Everything

When working with high heat and multiple dishes, having everything within reach can make all the difference. Side tables allow you to set your tools, seasonings, or plates without running back and forth to your kitchen. A storage box for your accessories ensures that everything stays organized, so you're not scrambling to find a spatula or thermometer while cooking. By keeping your grilling area clean and clutter-free, you can focus on what really matters—creating great food.

BBQ Gloves and Basting Brush: Safety and Flavor Control

Grilling often involves high temperatures, so safety is critical. A good pair of BBQ gloves will protect your hands from burns, allowing you to handle hot tools or adjust grates without worry. Meanwhile, a silicone basting brush ensures that marinades and sauces are applied evenly, essential for getting those rich, layered flavors into your food. These small but essential tools ensure that your cooking takes care of safety and flavor.

Grill Cover: Protecting Your Investment

A grill cover is essential for extending the life of your Pit Boss. It protects your equipment from rain, snow, dust, and UV rays, ensuring your grill stays in top shape for years.

Pellet Storage: Keep Your Fuel Ready

Storing your wood pellets in a dedicated pellet storage box keeps them dry and clean, ensuring consistent heat and flavor for your grill.

Cleaning Tools: Maintain Your Grill for Peak Performance

To keep your Pit Boss grill in top condition, use a heavy-duty grill brush and scraper to remove stuck-on food and grease. Grill-specific cleaners can help break down grease and grime. Regular maintenance with the right tools extends the life of your grill and ensures flavorful, consistent meals.

Ultimately, these accessories aren't just optional extras—they're essential elements that elevate your Pit Boss Wood Pellet Grill and Smoker experience. From precision tools like digital thermometers to safety essentials like BBQ gloves, each one plays a vital role in ensuring your grilling process is smooth and organized and, most importantly, delivers mouthwatering results every time. Investing in these accessories isn't just about making your life easier—it's about taking your cooking skills to the next level, ensuring that every dish you create reflects your dedication and expertise.

Preparing your Pit Boss Wood Pellet Grill and Smoker for its first use is not a one-time task. It's a crucial step in ensuring the long-term performance of your grill and the flavorful, smoky taste it will give your food. While some new grill owners might be tempted to skip or rush through this process, doing it properly ensures that your grill will operate efficiently and safely for years. The initial firing process helps to remove any oils or residues left from the manufacturing process, which could otherwise affect the grill's performance and the taste of your food. Like seasoning a cast iron skillet, this process creates a protective, non-stick layer on the grill's interior surfaces. This not only extends the life of your grill but also enhances the flavor of your food and prevents sticking, even during long, slow cooks. By taking the time to correctly fire and season your grill, you establish the foundation for that distinct, mouthwatering flavor that only a well-maintained pellet grill can provide.

Here's how to get started:

Step 1: Preparing for the Initial Firing

Before turning on your Pit Boss for the first time, do a quick safety check:

- **Inspect the Setup**: Ensure your grill is assembled correctly and placed in an open, well-ventilated area. Please keep it away from anything flammable, like overhanging branches, structures, or furniture.
- **Load the Hopper**: Fill the hopper with high-quality wood pellets. Don't stress too much about which flavor of pellets to use for this first burn; any standard wood pellets will do the trick.
- **Power It Up**: Plug your grill into a power source and switch it on. Set the temperature to the "Smoke" setting. This setting activates the drill, which starts feeding pellets into the firepot.

Step 2: Igniting the Grill

Once the pellets have begun to drop into the firepot, you'll hear them ignite, usually after a few minutes. The appearance of smoke is a good sign! It means that the ignition process is working correctly.

- **Raise the Temperature**: After the initial ignition, crank up the heat. Set your grill to the highest temperature setting. This step is crucial because it will burn off any leftover oils or chemicals used during manufacturing.
- **Monitor the Burn**: Let your Pit Boss run at this high temperature for 30 to 45 minutes. During this time, you may notice the smoke being a bit thicker and smelling different at first—that's just the leftover factory residues burning off. Over time, the smoke should take on the familiar, clean aroma of burning wood pellets.

Step 3: Cooling Down and Prepare for Seasoning

Once your grill has been running at high heat for the recommended time, it's time to shut it down. Follow the manufacturer's guidelines for shutting off the grill. Typically, this involves setting the control knob to the "Shut Down" position, which allows the fan to run and cool down the firepot safely.

Step 4: The Seasoning Process

After thoroughly cooling your grill from the initial firing, you can begin the seasoning process. This step is where you'll develop that essential non-stick surface on the grates and interior and lay the foundation for the signature flavor your grill will impart to every meal.

- **Coating with Oil**: Grab a bottle of high smoke point oil, such as canola, grapeseed, or even avocado oil. Using a cloth or paper towel, lightly coat the grates, the interior walls, and any other exposed metal parts inside the grill. Be generous, but don't overdo it—a thin, even layer is all you need. Why high smoke-point oil? These oils can withstand higher temperatures without breaking down, which is essential for forming a strong, durable seasoning layer.
- **Heat it Up Again**: Once you've oiled everything down, fire up your grill again. This time, set the temperature to around 350°F to 400°F. Let the grill run for about 45 minutes to an hour. During this time, the oil will bake into the metal, creating a protective, non-stick layer that's essential for preventing food from sticking and for easier cleaning in the future.
- **Repeat the Process**: You might want to repeat the oiling and heating process once or twice for the best results. The more you season your grill, the better the surface will be for cooking. Each layer adds to the non-stick properties and flavor-enhancing abilities of your grill.

Step 5: Inspect and Final Cool Down

Once the grill has completed its seasoning cycle, let it cool down again. Open the lid and inspect the surfaces. They should now have a darker, shiny appearance, indicating that the oil has baked adequately onto the metal.

Correctly firing and seasoning your Pit Boss is essential for great flavor and extending its life. As you use it more, the seasoning improves, enhancing future grilling sessions. Give your grill the love and attention it needs for years of mouthwatering cookouts!

Mastering the art of grilling with your Pit Boss Wood Pellet Grill and Smoker isn't just about following recipes—It's about understanding how temperature control and smoke management work together to create extraordinary flavors. These two key elements are at the heart of great barbecue, and learning to manage them effectively will set you on the path to grilling perfection. Let's dive into how you can harness the power of both to consistently deliver mouthwatering results every time you fire up your Pit Boss.

The Role of Temperature: Precision for Perfect Results

When it comes to grilling or smoking, temperature is the most critical factor affecting your food's texture, moisture, and flavor. Whether cooking a thick ribeye or slow-smoking a pork shoulder, maintaining the right temperature makes all the difference. A steady, well-controlled temperature helps your food cook evenly, prevents dryness, and ensures you achieve that perfect crust or tender, juicy interior.

One of the best things you can do is preheating your Pit Boss. Preheating stabilizes the cooking environment and helps you reach your desired cooking temperatures faster and more efficiently. You may need to adjust your temperatures depending on what you're grilling or smoking. For instance, if you're searing steaks, you'll want to crank the heat to around 450°F 500°F for that beautiful crust. On the other hand, if you're smoking a brisket, you'll want to keep the heat low and slow, at around 225°F to 250°F.

Navigating External Conditions: The Unseen Variables

One thing many people overlook is the impact of external factors on your grill's performance. Wind, humidity, and even the amount of food you cook can affect your grill's ability to maintain consistent heat. That's why monitoring and adjusting your temperature as conditions change is critical. Pit Boss models with Wi-Fi connectivity and programmable settings can be helpful here. You can adjust the temperature through an app without standing by the grill. This feature gives you a level of control that older models or traditional charcoal grills can't match.

These technological advances let you monitor your grill's temperature remotely, adjust the heat if needed, and keep your cooking on track, even if you're multitasking. It's a game-changer for those who want the flexibility to prepare meals while still being able to step away and enjoy the party.

The Magic of Smoke: Infusing Flavor Into Every Bite

Temperature control may ensure the correct doneness, but smoke takes your grilled dishes to the next level regarding flavor. Smoke introduces those deep, rich, and complex notes that define great barbecue.

It's important to remember that managing your smoker's vents is essential for controlling how much smoke interacts with your food. When the vents are more open, there's better airflow and lighter smoke, which can prevent your food from getting too much smoke. On the other hand, if you close the vents slightly, you'll get a thicker, more intense smoke, which is perfect for meats like brisket or ribs that benefit from a more potent flavor infusion.

Targeting the Perfect Doneness: Internal Temperature Guidelines

Knowing the ideal internal temperatures for different types of meat is essential for achieving the perfect level of doneness. For example, cooking beef to an internal temperature of 130°F will give you a perfect medium-rare. Poultry should reach at least 165°F to ensure it's safe to eat, while pork benefits from being pulled off the grill at around 145°F for a juicy, tender result. But beyond reaching these target temperatures, it's essential to maintain them consistently over time.

Pit Boss grills are equipped with built-in probes and PID (Proportional-Integral-Derivative) controllers, which continuously monitor and adjust the temperature for you. These features take much of the guesswork out of grilling and smoking, ensuring that the meat stays at the right temperature and cooks evenly from edge to center. This is especially important when dealing with more significant cuts of meat that must be simmered over several hours.

Balancing Heat and Smoke for Ultimate Control

The dance between temperature and smoke is where true mastery happens. While high heat is excellent for searing and quick cooking, low heat combined with just the right amount of smoke will work wonders for tougher cuts that need time to tenderize. The key to perfecting this balance is practice. Every cut of meat reacts differently, and external factors like wind or rain can throw a wrench in your plans. But once you've dialed in your settings for specific meats and conditions, you can replicate those results repeatedly.

At its core, controlling temperature and smoke isn't just about technical know-how—it's about understanding how your grill works and how different variables come together to create incredible meals. With the right balance of heat and smoke, along with the versatility of your Pit Boss, you'll be able to turn simple ingredients into delicious, unforgettable dishes.

> " The grill is the canvas, the meat is the art

Taking care of your Pit Boss Wood Pellet Grill and Smoker isn't just about keeping it looking good—it's essential for ensuring you get the best performance every time you fire it up. Regular maintenance goes a long way in preserving your grill's efficiency and extending its life so you can enjoy countless grilling sessions without hiccups. In this chapter, we'll walk you through the essential steps to keep your Pit Boss in top shape, with easy-to-follow cleaning and maintenance tips to ensure it's always ready for action.

After Each Use: Keeping Things Clean

The best way to ensure your Pit Boss stays in excellent condition is to clean it after each use. This prevents buildup that can affect its performance and keeps things running smoothly. Here's what you need to do every time you finish grilling:

- **Grill Grates**: Use a grill brush to scrub off any leftover food or grease after cooling the grates. You can also soak the grates in warm, soapy water, scrub them with a sponge or brush, rinse, and let them dry before putting them back.
- **Fire Pot**: Regularly remove ash and debris from the fire pot for efficient ignition and a cleaner burn. Use a shop vac after each use, especially after long grilling sessions.
- **Grease Tray**: Remember to empty the grease tray after every use and wipe it with warm, soapy water to prevent flare-ups and grease fires.

Weekly and Monthly Maintenance: Stay Ahead of Problems

Some tasks don't need to be done every time you use your grill, but keeping up with them weekly or monthly can prevent minor issues from becoming big headaches. Here's what to check:

- **Interior Surfaces**: Don't forget to clean the inside of your grill once a week to ensure even heat distribution and great flavor.
- **Pellet Hopper**: Moisture is the enemy of pellets. Inspect your pellet hopper monthly for moisture or dust buildup, which can cause jams. If you find any, empty the hopper and wipe it out to keep your pellets dry and flowing freely.
- **Seals and Gaskets**: Check your grill's seals and gaskets every few months and replace them if needed. Good seals ensure better temperature control and consistent cooking.
- **Auger System**: The drill delivers pellets to the fire pot; any blockage here can cause problems. Inspect the auger for buildup or blockages every month or so and clean it out to ensure smooth pellet delivery.

Annual Deep Cleaning: Give Your Grill Some TLC

Once a year, it's time for a deeper clean. This is where you'll disassemble some parts and give your grill a more thorough inspection:

- **Disassemble and Clean Critical Components**: Take apart crucial parts like the burn pot, diffuser plate, and grates and scrub them well. Check for damage or wear and replace any parts if needed.
- **Electrical Components**: Ensure all electrical components are dry and adequately connected during cleaning. A quick check can prevent future issues.
- **Tighten Hardware**: Over time, screws and bolts can loosen up from regular use. Tighten any loose hardware to keep your grill sturdy and reliable.

Extra Tips for Longevity

- **Prevent Rust**: After cleaning, apply a light oil coating to prevent rust and keep your grill in good condition, especially if exposed to the elements.
- **Storage**: When not in use, cover and store your grill in a dry place to protect it from weather damage and keep everything in working order for future use.
- **Pellet Quality:** Always use high-quality pellets for the best performance. Avoid cheap or old pellets as they can produce more ash and affect the taste of your food. Fresh, high-quality pellets burn cleaner and leave less residue behind.
- **Ventilation:** Regularly check and clean your grill's ventilation system to maintain airflow and consistent cooking temperatures.

Smoker Care: Keeping Your Smoker Clean

If you're using the smoker function on your Pit Boss, keeping it clean is just as important. After every smoking session:

- **Empty the Smoker Box**: Get rid of any leftover wood chips and ash.
- **Wash the Racks and Trays**: Use warm, soapy water to clean the cooking racks, water pan, and drip tray. After washing, dry them thoroughly and lightly oil the racks to prevent sticking next time.
- **Clean the Meat Probe**: Wipe down the meat probe with a damp cloth to ensure it stays accurate for your subsequent use.

Sticking to a cleaning and maintenance routine will not only extend the life of your Pit Boss but also ensure that every meal you cook is as delicious as the last. With regular care, your grill will continue to be your trusty companion for all your outdoor cooking adventures, delivering top-notch performance and mouthwatering results for years.

Even with regular cleaning and maintenance, you might encounter occasional hiccups when using your Pit Boss Wood Pellet Grill and Smoker. Don't worry—most issues can be easily fixed with some troubleshooting. This chapter will cover some of the users' most common problems and provide practical solutions to get your grill back up and running smoothly.

Grill Won't Ignite

One of the most frustrating issues is when your grill won't light up. There are several reasons for this, and the solution will depend on the underlying cause.

- Check the Pellet Hopper: The first thing to do is check the pellet hopper. If it's empty or if the pellets are stuck, they won't feed into the auger, and your grill won't be able to ignite. Ensure the hopper has enough pellets, and clear any jams that might prevent them from feeding.
- Inspect the Fire Pot: Sometimes, ash or residue can build up in the fire pot, blocking the igniter. If so, vacuum the fire pot to ensure proper airflow and ignition. It's also worth checking to ensure the igniter works by looking for the red glow in the fire pot when you try to start the grill.
- Test the Power Supply: Ensure your grill is properly plugged in and the outlet functions. If you're using an extension cord, double-check that it's rated for outdoor use and has the correct wattage to power the grill.

Grill Temperature Fluctuates

If your Pit Boss isn't maintaining a steady temperature, it could be due to various factors. Here are a few things to check:

- Pellet Quality: Low-quality or moist pellets can lead to inconsistent burns, which affects the grill's temperature stability. Always store pellets in a dry place and ensure you use high-quality, fresh pellets to keep the heat consistent.
- Clean the Grill: The buildup of ash and grease inside the grill can obstruct airflow, causing temperature fluctuations. Ensure the fire pot, grates, and internal surfaces are clean for optimal performance.
- Check the Thermometer: If the built-in thermometer gives incorrect readings, it may need recalibration. Use a digital meat probe or grill thermometer to cross-check the temperature and ensure accuracy.
- Wind and Weather Conditions: Wind, rain, and extreme cold can affect the grill's ability to maintain a consistent temperature. If you're grilling in harsh conditions, consider using a grill blanket or moving the grill to a more sheltered area.

Pellets Aren't Feeding Properly

A common issue Pit Boss owners face is when pellets aren't feeding into the fire pot correctly. This usually leads to the grill failing to maintain temperature or not igniting.

- Check for Pellet Jams: Pellet jams can happen if the pellets are too long or if moisture builds up in the hopper. Inspect the auger and hopper to make sure the pellets are feeding smoothly. If you notice a jam, use a tool to gently free up the drill and remove the blockage.
- Inspect the Auger Motor: If the drill isn't turning, the motor could malfunction. First, unplug the grill, then inspect the wiring and connections to ensure everything is secure. If the motor still doesn't work, it may need to be replaced.
- Keep Pellets Dry: Moist pellets can clump together and cause feeding issues. Always store your pellets in a dry place; if you suspect they've absorbed moisture, it's best to replace them with fresh pellets.

Grease Fires or Excessive Smoke

Grease fires are rare but can occur if too much grease accumulates inside the grill. Additionally, excessive smoke could be a sign of improper cleaning or pellet issues.

- Clean the Grease Tray and Fire Pot: Grease fires typically happen when fat and oil collect in the grease tray or fire pot. Be sure to empty and clean these components regularly to prevent flare-ups. For smoke issues, excessive ash buildup can block airflow and cause incomplete combustion, resulting in thick, dirty smoke.
- Check Pellet Quality: Excessive smoke can also result from poor-quality pellets or pellets that aren't burning efficiently. Always use premium-grade hardwood pellets to achieve clean, consistent smoke.

Uneven Cooking

If you find that some areas of your grill are hotter than others, you may experience uneven cooking, which can be frustrating. This could happen for several reasons:

- Check the Grill's Interior: Uneven heat distribution could be due to a buildup of ash or grease on the diffuser plate or internal surfaces. Clean the interior thoroughly to ensure proper airflow and heat distribution across the grill.
- Arrange Food Properly: Overloading the grill or placing Food too closely together can block airflow, leading to uneven cooking. Ensure enough space between the items to allow air to circulate evenly.
- Rotate the Food: If one side of your Food is cooking faster than the other, try rotating it halfway through the cooking process. This can help with heat exposure and give you a more consistent result.

TROUBLESHOOTING COMMON ISSUES

Grill Shuts Off Mid-Cook

If your Pit Boss shuts off unexpectedly during cooking, it can disrupt your meal and affect the grill's overall performance.

- Check the Power Source: Ensure the grill is correctly connected to a reliable power source. Power surges, faulty outlets, or loose plugs can cause the grill to shut off unexpectedly. If you're using an extension cord, ensure it's in good condition and rated for the grill's power needs.
- Inspect the Auger System: If the auger gets jammed, the grill may shut down as a safety measure. Clear any blockages in the auger and check that the pellets feed smoothly into the fire pot.

Grill Won't Reach High Temperatures

Sometimes, your Pit Boss may need help to reach high temperatures, which can be frustrating if you're trying to sear or cook at higher heat settings.

- Inspect the Airflow: Blockages in the ventilation system can prevent the grill from reaching high temperatures. Ensure all air vents are clear, and clean out the fire pot and chimney to allow proper airflow.
- Use Fresh Pellets: Old or damp pellets may burn less efficiently, making it difficult for the grill to reach higher temperatures. Make sure your pellets are fresh and dry for optimal heat performance.

Overheating Issues

If your grill is overheating, it can affect the food and potentially damage the unit. Here's how to handle it:

- Reduce Pellet Feed: If the grill temperature is climbing too high, the first step is to reduce the pellets' feed rate. This can be done by adjusting the temperature settings to lower the rate at which pellets are fed into the fire pot.
- Check for Air Leaks: Sometimes, overheating is caused by air leaks in the grill's seals or gaskets. Inspect the door seals and lid to ensure they're intact and aren't allowing excess air into the grill. Excess air can cause the pellets to burn hotter and faster, leading to temperature spikes.
- Avoid Opening the Lid Frequently: Continuously opening the grill lid can cause temperature swings, as the grill compensates for the sudden influx of cooler air by heating up quickly when the lid is closed again. Try to minimize the number of times you open the grill during cooking to keep the temperature steady.
- Ventilation Control: If your grill has a chimney or vent, check that it's not fully closed. A closed vent can trap too much heat, causing the grill to overheat. Adjust the vent to allow for proper airflow.

Dry or Overcooked Meat

Dry, overcooked meat can be a significant disappointment, but with a few adjustments, you can prevent this from happening:

- Use a Meat Probe: Always rely on a meat probe or digital thermometer to monitor the internal temperature of the meat. Cooking on time alone can lead to overcooked meat, especially for cuts like steak or pork chops, which cook quickly. Aim for the recommended internal temperatures for the type of meat you're cooking.
- Consider Indirect Cooking: If you're grilling a large piece of meat, like brisket or pork shoulder, try using indirect heat to slow the cooking process. This helps avoid drying out the meat's exterior while ensuring the inside is cooked correctly.
- Baste or Use a Butter Drip: To keep moisture in the meat, consider basting it periodically with its own juices, butter, or another fat source. This not only helps lock in moisture but also enhances flavor.
- Control the Heat: High-heat cooking can lead to dry meat on the outside and undercooked inside. For cuts that benefit from slower cooking, reduce the temperature slightly to allow the meat to cook evenly, maintaining its juices.

By troubleshooting these common issues, you can keep your Pit Boss running smoothly and ensure your grilling experience is as enjoyable as possible. With some know-how and regular care, most problems can be solved quickly, allowing you to focus on what matters most—creating delicious meals!

> Grilling is not just cooking; it's an alchemy. Transforming meat into gold, one flame-kissed piece at a time

Safety is essential when working with a wood pellet smoker and grill. These devices can reach incredibly high temperatures, so taking the proper precautions can protect you, your home, and your loved ones from accidents. The blend of modern technology and traditional wood-fired flavor offers a unique cooking experience, but it also calls for a tailored approach to safety.

In this chapter, we'll discuss key safety measures to follow before, during, and after grilling to ensure a safe, enjoyable, and delicious cookout every time.

Setting Up for Success: Preparing Your Space

Clear Your Cooking Area
Before you even fire up the grill:
- Make sure your setup is safe.
- Start by positioning your smoker on a stable, non-flammable surface.
- Avoid placing it near anything that could catch fire, like dry grass, wooden structures, or outdoor furniture made of flammable materials.

This simple step reduces the risk of accidental fires due to heat or sparks from your grill.

Establish a Safe Zone for Pets and Children
Pets and kids are naturally curious, but their excitement can lead to accidents around a hot grill. Set up a "no-go" zone—ideally, a perimeter of at least three feet around the smoker. Let everyone know to steer clear of this area while the grill is on and even after you've turned it off, as residual heat can linger.

Grilling Time: Staying Safe While Cooking

Monitor the Grill Constantly
Once your grill is fired up, keeping a close eye on it is crucial. The flame in a wood pellet smoker can be more complex than a traditional grill, making it easier to detect flare-ups or issues immediately. Stay near the grill throughout the cooking process to avoid food catching fire or embers escaping and igniting nearby objects.

Use the Right Tools
Grilling tools aren't just for flipping burgers but for keeping you safe. Always opt for long-handled utensils to keep your hands and face at a safe distance from the heat. Tongs and spatulas designed for grilling allow you to turn food without getting too close to the flames.

Wear Protective Gear
Wearing the proper clothing can make a big difference in preventing burns. Avoid loose-fitting clothes that could catch fire or dangle near the heat. Instead, opt for snug, long-sleeved shirts and long pants to protect your skin. Silicone or heat-resistant gloves are another must-have, providing extra protection when handling hot surfaces.

Fire Prevention and Control

Never Leave Your Grill Unattended
High heat can escalate situations quickly, especially when grilling fatty cuts of meat that may cause flare-ups. Always stay nearby to keep things under control. If you need to step away, have someone else take over or lower the temperature to reduce the risk of flames getting out of hand.

Keep a Fire Extinguisher Nearby
Grease fires are among the most common hazards when grilling, and you should be ready to handle them. Keep a fire extinguisher or a box of baking soda within arm's reach. If a grease fire does occur, never use water—it can make the fire worse. Instead, smother it with baking soda or use the extinguisher to put it out quickly.

Regularly Check for Gas Leaks (For Hybrid Grills)
Safety checks are even more crucial if you use a hybrid grill that operates on wood pellets and gas. Make it a habit to inspect hoses and connections for leaks before starting up the grill. A quick way to check for leaks is to use a soap and water solution—bubbles will form if gas is escaping.

Maintenance: Ensuring a Safe and Long-Lasting Grill

Clean the Grill After Every Use
Grill maintenance isn't just about keeping your food tasting great—it's a crucial part of staying safe. After each use, thoroughly clean the grill to prevent grease buildup, which can easily catch fire the next time you cook. Scrape the grates, empty the smoker box, and wipe down all surfaces to remove leftover grease or debris.

Deep Clean Regularly
Beyond daily cleaning, your grill needs regular deep maintenance to perform at its best and stay safe. Check for buildup in critical areas like the fire pot, auger system, and grease management trays. If they become clogged, these parts are most likely to cause issues.

Store Properly When Not in Use
When your grilling session ends, don't leave the smoker in the elements. Cover it with a grill cover or store it in a sheltered area. This protects it from rust and wear and reduces the chance of electrical malfunctions caused by moisture or weather damage.

Operational Tips: Cooking Safely

Keep Temperatures in Check

Using a grill thermometer isn't just for perfecting your steak—it's also an essential safety tool. Excessive heat can lead to out-of-control flames, ruined food, and increased fire risk. You can prevent these issues and cook more efficiently by monitoring the temperature closely.

Ensure Proper Ventilation

Grills need space to breathe. Ensure your smoker is positioned in an open, well-ventilated area, away from walls, fences, or overhanging structures. Adequate airflow helps the grill function properly and prevents heat from building up in unwanted places, which could cause structural damage or increase fire risk.

Choose Quality Wood Pellets

Low-quality or damp pellets can result in uneven burning, excessive smoke, and even fire hazards. Always opt for high-quality, dry pellets to ensure a clean, steady burn that minimizes these risks.

After Cooking: Proper Care and Cleaning

Let the Grill Cool Down Completely

Once you're done cooking, resist the urge to immediately start cleaning or moving the grill. Wait until the grill has cooled completely before doing anything. Handling hot parts can lead to severe burns, and cleaning while hot can damage the grill.

Use Gentle Cleaning Solutions

When it's time to clean, stick to non-abrasive solutions. Harsh chemicals can damage the surfaces of your grill, and water should be avoided around electrical components. For stubborn residue, a simple mix of vinegar or baking soda often does the trick without causing harm.

Following these safety tips doesn't just protect you—it prolongs the life of your grill. By cleaning and maintaining your smoker regularly and practicing safe grilling habits, you'll enjoy countless seasons of delicious, wood-fired meals. Safety and care are the keys to mastering the art of wood pellet cooking and ensuring every grilling session is as enjoyable as it is flavorful.

GRILLING: TECHNIQUES AND TIPS

Mastering the art of grilling involves learning two essential techniques: **direct** and **indirect**. Each method harnesses heat uniquely, and knowing when to use each technique can elevate your grilling game to new heights.

The Science Behind Heat Transfer

To become skilled at grilling, it's essential to grasp how heat moves during cooking. Direct grilling uses radiant heat, which is the direct transfer of energy from the heat source—whether it's charcoal, gas, or wood—straight to your food. This high-intensity heat sears the outside of your food, giving it that perfect grill mark and delicious crust.

Indirect grilling, on the other hand, works more like an oven. Here, heat circulates around your food rather than hitting it directly. This method uses lower, more controlled temperatures, allowing food to cook evenly from all sides without the risk of burning or over-charring. The circulating heat (convection) in your grill envelops the food, ensuring it gets cooked thoroughly, especially when dealing with more extensive or brutal cuts of meat.

Direct Grilling: Quick and Intense

Direct grilling is all about speed and high heat. With temperatures ranging from 400°F to 550°F, it's the method to use when cooking minor, more tender cuts of meat like steaks, chops, chicken breasts, or vegetables that don't need a long time to cook. The intense heat causes the Maillard reaction—a fancy term for the chemical reaction that happens when amino acids and sugars in the food interact under high temperatures. This process is what gives your food that beautiful, savory brown crust.

At the same time, caramelization is happening. The natural sugars in your food break down and form new compounds, creating that sweet, nutty flavor we all love in grilled veggies or meats. These two processes —Maillard reaction and caramelization—are crucial for giving grilled foods their characteristic flavor and texture. However, with direct grilling, you have to keep a close eye on things. Because the heat is so high, it's easy for food to go from perfectly seared to burnt in no time. Stay vigilant to avoid unwanted charring, which can produce bitter flavors.

Indirect Grilling: Slow and Steady

Indirect grilling is the technique you'll want to use for more extensive, thicker cuts of meat like ribs, brisket, whole chicken, or roasts. Instead of placing your food directly over the flames, you'll cook it off to the side, using the grill more like a smoker or an oven. Temperatures are lower, typically between 225°F and 325°F, which allows the meat to cook slowly and evenly.

One of the great benefits of indirect grilling is that it allows tougher cuts of meat to break down gradually. As the meat slowly reaches an internal temperature above 160°F, the collagen in the connective tissue starts to break down into gelatin. This process is what gives slow-cooked meats that melt-in-your-mouth, fall-off-the-bone tenderness.

Another bonus of indirect grilling is that it allows you to incorporate smoke for flavor. Whether you're using wood chips, pellets, or chunks, the slower cooking process ensures the food absorbs that rich, smoky flavor. Smoke particles, which contain compounds like phenols and carbonyls, adhere to the surface of the food, infusing it with layers of complex flavors. This is something you can't achieve with high-heat direct grilling.

By mastering the differences between direct and indirect grilling, you'll be well on your way to becoming a more confident, versatile grill master. Knowing when to apply each method will ensure you get the most flavor and tenderness from everything you cook, making your grilling sessions a hit every time.

When you combine the timeless techniques of smoking, roasting, and baking with the versatility of the Pit Boss Wood Pellet Grill, the result is nothing short of culinary magic. These three methods cook your food and can transform it, enhancing flavors, textures, and aromas. Whether smoking a rack of ribs, roasting a whole chicken, or baking a casserole, the Pit Boss offers precision and ease. In this chapter, we'll explore the science and art behind each method with practical tips and expanded insights into achieving the best results every time.

Smoking: Infusing Deep Flavor with Patience and Precision

Smoking is a slow-cooking method that imparts a rich, smoky flavor to meats, fish, and vegetables. When you smoke food on the Pit Boss, you're not just cooking it but infusing it with layers of flavor from the wood pellets. The smoke, produced by the slow burning of these pellets, penetrates deep into the food, giving it a robust and complex characteristic taste.

The Pit Boss uses wood pellets made from compressed sawdust, which are burned slowly to create a controlled and consistent heat. Smoking involves chemical processes such as the Maillard reaction (browning and caramelization of the surface) and pyrolysis (breakdown of wood into aromatic compounds), resulting in the rich flavors of smoked foods.

Specific cuts of meat are particularly well-suited for smoking because of their fat content and texture. Here's a quick guide:

- Pork Shoulder/Boston Butt: Perfect for pulled pork, this cut benefits from prolonged, slow smoking to break down the fat and connective tissue, resulting in tender, juicy meat.
- Beef Brisket: Another favorite for smoking, brisket needs low heat over a long period to achieve the desired tenderness and rich flavor.
- Whole Chicken or Turkey: Poultry absorbs smoke flavor well and can remain moist, especially when smoked at a lower temperature over several hours.

The type of wood pellets you use can significantly affect the flavor of your food. Each wood imparts its own unique set of aromas:

- Hickory: Offers a strong, smoky, bacon-like flavor that pairs well with beef and pork.
- Applewood: A sweeter, lighter smoke ideal for poultry and fish, adding a delicate touch without overpowering the natural flavor.
- Mesquite: Known for its bold, earthy flavor, mesquite is best for more robust meats like beef or game.

Roasting: Achieving the Perfect Crust and Juicy Interior

Roasting is all about balance: getting that golden, caramelized exterior while ensuring the inside stays juicy and tender. With the Pit Boss's precise temperature control, roasting becomes an almost hands-off process, allowing you to achieve perfect results every time. Roasting works well for meats, vegetables, and even fruits, leveraging dry heat to caramelize the natural sugars in the food.

Roasting is versatile, but specific cuts of meat excel when exposed to dry, indirect heat. Here are some recommendations:

- Whole Chicken: Roasting a whole chicken on the Pit Boss allows you to achieve crispy skin while keeping the meat juicy.
- Pork Loin: This lean cut can dry out quickly, but it remains tender and flavorful with careful roasting at a lower temperature.
- Beef Tenderloin: A premium cut, beef tenderloin benefits from high-heat roasting to develop a flavorful crust while keeping the center perfectly pink.

One of the critical advantages of roasting with the Pit Boss is the ability to set and maintain a precise temperature. For most roasts, you'll want to aim for:

- High heat (375°F to 425°F) is great for quickly browning and caramelizing the exterior of meats and vegetables while keeping the inside moist.
- Moderate heat (300°F to 350°F) is ideal for larger cuts of meat that need time to cook through, like a whole turkey or prime rib.

To retain moisture while roasting, you can use techniques like basting with melted butter or drippings or placing a shallow pan of water or broth in the grill to create a more humid cooking environment. This will prevent the meat from drying out, especially during long roasting sessions.

Baking: From Bread to Casseroles, Done Outdoors

Yes, you can bake on the Pit Boss! Baking is often associated with indoor ovens, but the grill's enclosed space and even heat distribution make it a perfect outdoor oven. Baking involves lower, steadier temperatures than roasting and smoking, ideal for dishes that need gentle, even cooking.

The possibilities for baking on the grill are endless:
- Cornbread: The subtle infusion of smoke adds a unique twist to traditional cornbread.
- Casseroles: Whether for breakfast or a savory dinner,

baking casseroles on the grill adds a depth of flavor you can't get in a traditional oven.

- Bread: While bread might not be the first thing you think of baking on a grill, the Pit Boss can easily handle it, producing a crispy crust and soft interior.

For most baked goods, you'll want to keep the temperature between 300°F and 350°F, ensuring an even cook without burning the edges. The Pit Boss's ability to maintain a steady temperature means you don't have to worry about hot spots, a common issue in traditional ovens.

Combining Techniques: Smoking, Then Roasting for Optimal Flavor

One of the most thrilling ways to utilize your Pit Boss is by merging smoking and roasting methods. This blend can transform a meal from good to unforgettable. Start by smoking your meat at a low temperature to fill it with rich, smoky flavors, then finish it with a higher-temperature roast to create a caramelized crust.

Example of Technique Combination:

Pork Shoulder Smoked then Roasted: Commence by smoking the pork shoulder at 225°F for several hours, letting the smoke seep into the meat. Once it attains the desired level of smokiness, turn up the heat to 350°F to form a crispy exterior while retaining a tender, moist interior.

This fusion of methods provides the best of both worlds: the profound flavor of smoking and the ideal texture achieved through roasting.

Timing and Preparation: A Handy Guide for Smoking, Roasting, and Baking

For each technique, timing is critical to getting the best results. Here are some general guidelines for smoking, roasting, and baking popular items on your Pit Boss:

- Whole Chicken (Roasting): Roast at 375°F for about 1.5 to 2 hours, depending on the size of the bird, until the internal temperature reaches 165°F.
- Pork Ribs (Smoking): Smoke at 225°F for 5-6 hours, wrapping them in foil halfway through to retain moisture.
- Beef Brisket (Smoking): Plan for 1 to 1.5 hours per pound at 225°F, and don't rush—the brisket needs time to break down the connective tissue.
- Cornbread (Baking): Bake at 350°F for 20-25 minutes or until golden brown on top.

Each of these timing guidelines can be adjusted based on the size of the food, but the key takeaway is that patience and temperature control are crucial to getting the best results.

Smoking, roasting, and baking are foundational techniques in any grill master's toolkit, and the Pit Boss allows you to execute them with precision and ease. Understanding how these techniques work and experimenting with different cuts, temperatures, and wood pellet varieties will open up a world of culinary possibilities in your backyard.

Unlocking the full flavor potential of your food with wood pellets is a journey that combines art and science. At its core, smoking with wood pellets is rooted in the fascinating reaction known as pyrolysis, where heat breaks down wood without oxygen. This process releases gases, volatile compounds, and tiny solid particles we call smoke. But smoke is more than just a byproduct—it's a complex mix of compounds that imbue your food with rich, distinct flavors, depending on the wood you use.

The Science of Smoke: How Wood Enhances Flavor

Every type of wood has a unique flavor signature that is released when burned. The composition of smoke varies significantly based on the type of wood, and these variations make selecting the right wood pellet crucial for enhancing your food's flavor.

- *Phenols*: Aromatic compounds that give smoked foods their characteristic flavor. They also have antimicrobial properties, which historically helped preserve food before the advent of refrigeration. The deep, complex, smoky taste you associate with barbecue owes much of its flavor to phenols.
- *Guaiacol and Syringol*: These compounds are derivatives of phenols and are responsible for the distinctive smoky aroma. Guaiacol offers a spicy, sharp smoke note, while Syringol lends a sweeter, more subtle, smoky essence. Together, these two compounds work to make smoke not just a flavor enhancer but also an integral part of the grilling experience.
- *Carbonyls*: Responsible for the beautiful browning of your meats, carbonyls play a crucial role in the Maillard reaction, where proteins and sugars in the food react at high temperatures, developing deep, rich flavors. This also gives grilled or smoked meats their delicious crust and enhances their overall complexity.

The balance of these compounds in the smoke varies depending on the wood you're using. For example, hickory pellets create a robust, bacon-like flavor, perfect for heavier meats like pork and beef. At the same time, applewood releases a lighter, fruity smoke that works wonderfully with more delicate proteins like chicken and fish.

One often overlooked aspect of wood smoke is the condition of the wood itself. Wood's aging or staging—how long it has been dried before being made into pellets—can significantly impact the quality of smoke and the flavors it produces.

Well-aged wood creates cleaner, smoother smoke with less bitterness, while wood that is too green or not adequately dried can produce harsh, acrid flavors due to excessive moisture. The moisture causes incomplete combustion, which results in a less desirable smoky profile. So, when choosing wood pellets, ensure they come from well-seasoned wood for the best flavor results.

Hardwood vs. Softwood: Which is Better for Smoking?

Another critical consideration when selecting wood pellets is understanding the difference between hardwoods and softwoods. Hardwoods are generally preferred for smoking because they burn longer, produce more consistent heat and release more decadent flavors. Examples of hardwoods include oak, hickory, and maple, all of which are excellent choices for most smoked dishes.

Softwoods, such as pine or spruce, contain higher levels of resin, which can impart a bitter, unpleasant taste to food. For this reason, softwoods are generally avoided when grilling and smoking. Sticking to hardwood pellets ensures you get clean, flavorful smoke that enhances your food without overpowering it.

Smoke Time and Its Effect on Flavor

Another critical factor affecting your food's flavor is the time it absorbs smoke. The longer food is exposed to smoke, the smoky flavor intensifies. However, there's a fine line between enhancing flavor and overpowering it.

For instance, delicate foods like chicken or fish should not be smoked for as long as heartier meats like beef brisket or pork shoulder. The latter can handle extended smoking times, allowing the rich, intense flavors of woods like mesquite or hickory to develop fully. For lighter meats, a shorter smoking time with a milder wood, like apple or cherry, will yield the best results.

Blending Wood Pellets for Custom Flavor Profiles

Once you've mastered using single wood pellets, blending different woods opens up a new world of flavor possibilities. The beauty of blending is that you can create custom profiles to suit your taste or match specific dishes. For example, blending a bold wood like oak with a sweeter wood like cherry can create a balanced, rich, and mellow smoke.

Here's how you can start blending wood pellets for your grilling:

- Begin with Single Woods: Start by using one type of wood to get familiar with its flavor profile. Once you understand how each wood influences the flavor of your food, you can move on to blending.
- Blend Gradually: Start using a base wood, such as oak or hickory, and add small amounts of another wood, like apple or cherry, until you achieve the desired balance. You can fine-tune the ratio to adjust the intensity of the smoke and flavor.
- Taste and Adjust: After blending and grilling, conduct a taste test to evaluate how the combination of woods enhances the flavor of your food. Over time, you'll develop an instinct for how different woods interact and which combinations work best for different meats and dishes.

Exploring the Versatility of Wood Smoke

While smoking is traditionally associated with meat, wood smoke can enhance a variety of foods, including vegetables, cheeses, and even drinks. Many chefs have experimented with cold smoking to infuse foods with smoky flavors without cooking them. Cold-smoked cheeses, nuts, and even cocktails have gained popularity as creative applications of wood smoke, showing that the possibilities extend far beyond the grill.

In cold smoking, food is exposed to smoke at lower temperatures, infusing it with deep, rich flavors without altering its texture. For example, cold-smoking cheeses like cheddar or gouda add a smoky complexity that complements the creaminess of the cheese, making them a standout addition to any charcuterie board.

The Importance of Temperature Control

Temperature control is another vital aspect of smoking with wood pellets. The temperature at which the pellets burn can drastically affect the quality of the smoke and the flavor it imparts. Burning pellets at too high a temperature can produce thick, acrid smoke, which may leave a bitter aftertaste. On the other hand, maintaining a steady, moderate heat ensures a clean, aromatic smoke that enhances the food without overwhelming it.

To get the best results when smoking food, it's essential to carefully control the temperature of your smoker. This allows you to regulate the amount of smoke the food absorbs and ensures it cooks evenly. Slow and steady smoking is critical to developing rich flavors and achieving tender, perfectly cooked meat.

Storytelling and Tradition: The Art of Smoking

Smoking meat is more than just a cooking technique—it's a tradition steeped in history. Across the world, different cultures have used wood to preserve and flavor food for centuries. In the Appalachian Mountains, families would gather to smoke pork for winter storage, using wood from nearby forests to flavor the meat. The type of wood used was often dictated by what was locally available, and over time, these woods became synonymous with the distinct flavors of regional barbecue.

Grilling and smoking today carry on that legacy, allowing home cooks to tap into this rich culinary history. Whether you're smoking brisket in Texas with mesquite or crafting a Pacific Northwest salmon with alder, the wood you choose is a link to the past, connecting your grill to traditions that span generations.

MEAT RECIPES

Ingredients

- 4-5 lb beef brisket
- 2 tbsp kosher salt
- 2 tbsp coarse black pepper
- 1 tbsp garlic powder
- 1 tbsp onion powder
- 1 tbsp paprika
- 1 tsp cayenne pepper (optional for extra heat)
- 2 tbsp yellow mustard (for binding)
- Wood pellets: Hickory or Oak

SMOKED BEEF BRISKET

Directions

1. Prepare the Brisket: Trim excess fat, leaving a 1/4-inch fat cap for moisture.
2. Season the Brisket: Rub the brisket with mustard. Mix salt, pepper, garlic powder, onion powder, paprika, and cayenne. Coat the brisket thoroughly with the rub.
3. Marinate Overnight: Wrap the brisket in plastic wrap and refrigerate overnight.
4. Preheat the Pit Boss: Set your Pit Boss to 225°F with hickory or oak pellets.
5. Smoke the Brisket: Place the brisket fat side up and smoke for 4-5 hours until the internal temperature reaches 165°F.
6. Wrap the Brisket: Wrap in butcher paper or foil, return to the grill, and smoke until the internal temperature reaches 200-205°F (about 2-3 more hours).
7. Rest the Brisket: Let it rest wrapped for 1 hour before slicing against the grain.

Serves

4

Prep Time

20 min

(+ overnight marinating)

Cooking Time

6-8 hours

T I P S

- Hickory adds a robust and traditional BBQ flavor, while oak gives a milder, earthy smoke.
- Add 1 tbsp of brown sugar to the rub for a slightly sweet, caramelized crust.

28

HONEY GARLIC PORK CHOPS

Prep time: 15 min Cooking time: 90 min | Serves: 4

Ingredients

- 4 bone-in pork chops (about 1-inch thick)
- 1/4 cup honey
- 3 garlic cloves, minced
- 2 tbsp soy sauce
- 2 tbsp apple cider vinegar
- 1 tbsp olive oil
- 1 tsp black pepper
- 1 tsp kosher salt
- Wood pellets: Apple or Cherry

Directions

1. Prepare the Marinade: In a bowl, whisk together honey, minced garlic soy sauce, apple cider vinegar, olive oil, black pepper, and salt.
2. Marinate the Pork Chops: Place the pork chops in a resealable plastic bag or container. Pour the honey garlic marinade over the chops, ensuring they're well-coated. Marinate for at least 30 minutes (or up t 2 hours in the refrigerator for more flavor).
3. Preheat the Pit Boss: Set your Pit Boss to 225°F, using apple or cherr wood pellets for a mild, sweet-smoke flavor.
4. Smoke the Pork Chops: Remove the pork chops from the marinade (reserving some for basting) and place them on the grill. Smoke for 1 to 1.5 hours or until the internal temperature reaches 145°F.
5. Baste and Finish: In the last 10 minutes of cooking, baste the pork chops with the remaining marinade. Let the chops rest for 5-10 minutes before serving.

TIPS
- Apple or cherry wood gives a sweet, fruity smoke that pairs perfectly with the honey garlic glaze.
- Add 1/2 tsp of red pepper flakes to the marinade for a spicy kick.

SMOKED TURKEY BREAST

Prep time: 15 min | Cooking time: 3-4 hours | Serves: 4

Ingredients

- 1 boneless turkey breast (about 4 lbs)
- 2 tbsp olive oil
- 1 tbsp kosher salt
- 1 tbsp black pepper
- 1 tbsp garlic powder
- 1 tbsp paprika
- 1 tsp onion powder
- 1 tsp dried thyme
- 1/2 tsp cayenne pepper (optional)
- 1/2 cup unsalted butter, melted

Directions

1. Pat the turkey breast dry with paper towels. Rub the olive oil all over the turkey to help the seasoning stick.
2. Season the turkey breast with a mixture of kosher salt, black pepper, garlic powder, paprika, onion powder, dried thyme, and cayenne pepper (if using).
3. Set your Pit Boss Wood Pellet Grill to 225°F and use applewood or cherrywood pellets for a mild, sweet smoke that complements turkey perfectly.
4. Place the seasoned turkey breast on the smoker grates and insert a meat thermometer into the thickest part of the breast to monitor the temperature.
5. After the first hour of smoking, brush the turkey with melted butter every 45 minutes to moisten it and add flavor.
6. Smoke the turkey breast until it reaches 165°F, about 3-4 hours. Remove from smoker when done.
7. Let the breast rest for 10-15 minutes before slicing for a tender, juicy turkey.

TIPS
- Use applewood or cherrywood pellets for a sweet, mild smoke that enhances the turkey's natural flavors without overpowering them.
- Turn the grill to 375°F during the last 15 minutes to crisp up the skin.

Ingredients

- 2 racks of St. Louis Style Spare Ribs (around 4-5 lbs total)
- 2 tbsp yellow mustard
- ¼ cup pork dry rub (your favorite blend or store-bought)
- 1 cup apple juice (for spritzing)
- 1 cup barbecue sauce (optional for glazing)
- 2 tbsp brown sugar (optional for added sweetness)

Serves

4

Prep Time

15 min

Cooking Time

5-5 hours

SMOKED ST. LOUIS STYLE SPARE RIBS

Directions

1. Prepare the Ribs: Remove the membrane from the back of the ribs by sliding a knife under it and pulling it off.
2. Apply the Rub: Coat both sides of the ribs with yellow mustard and add the pork dry rub, pressing it into the meat.
3. Preheat the Pit Boss: Set your Pit Boss to 225°F, fill the hopper with hickory or applewood pellets, and let the grill come to temperature before placing the ribs inside.
4. Begin Smoking: Place the rib bone on the grill and smoke at 225°F for 3 hours without opening the lid.
5. Spritz the Ribs: After 3 hours, spritz with apple juice every 30 minutes for 2-3 hours.
6. Check for Doneness: After 5 hours, check the ribs for tenderness. The meat should pull back from the bones, and the internal temperature should be around 190-203°F. If needed, smoke for an additional 30-60 minutes.
7. Optional Glaze: For a sticky, sweet finish, brush the ribs with barbecue sauce, sprinkle with brown sugar, and cook for 15-20 minutes to set the glaze.
8. Rest and Serve: After smoking, let the ribs rest for 10-15 minutes before slicing. Serve as-is or with extra barbecue sauce.

T I P S

- For a spicier kick, add cayenne to your dry rub or glaze with honey for sweetness.
- Use hickory wood for a bold, smoky flavor or applewood for a sweeter, milder smoke that complements the pork perfectly.

GRILLED LAMB CHOPS WITH HERB MARINADE

Prep time: 10 min
+ 2 h marinating time

Cooking time: 15 min

Serves: 4

Ingredients

- 8 lamb chops (about 1 inch thick)
- ¼ cup olive oil
- 2 tbsp fresh rosemary, chopped
- 2 tbsp fresh thyme, chopped
- 4 garlic cloves, minced
- 1 tsp lemon zest
- 1 tbsp lemon juice
- 1 tsp salt
- ½ tsp black pepper

Directions

1. Prepare the Marinade: In a bowl, mix together olive oil, rosemary, thyme, garlic, lemon zest, lemon juice, salt, and pepper.
2. Marinate the Lamb Chops: Place the lamb chops in a large resealable bag or shallow dish. Pour the marinade over the chops, ensuring they are evenly coated. Seal the bag or cover the dish, then refrigerate for at least 2 hours (or overnight for deeper flavor).
3. Preheat the Pit Boss: Set your Pit Boss to 400°F and use oak or cherrywood pellets for smoking. Let the grill preheat for about 10 minutes.
4. Grill the Lamb Chops: Remove the lamb chops from the marinade, allowing excess to drip off. Place the chops directly on the grill grates and cook for 4-5 minutes per side for medium-rare or until the internal temperature reaches 135°F.
5. Rest and Serve: Remove the lamb chops from the grill and let them rest for 5 minutes before serving. This allows the juices to be redistributed for maximum flavor.

TIPS
- For extra flavor, drizzle a balsamic glaze on top when serving.
- Use oak pellets for a robust, earthy smoke or cherrywood for a sweetness that enhances the herbs and lamb.

TANGY BBQ TURKEY LEGS

Prep time: 10 min
+ 1 h marinating time

Cooking time: 2-3 hours

Serves: 4

Ingredients

- 4 large turkey legs
- 1 cup barbecue sauce (your favorite brand or homemade)
- ¼ cup apple cider vinegar
- 2 tbsp olive oil
- 1 tbsp smoked paprika
- 1 tsp garlic powder
- 1 tsp onion powder
- 1 tsp black pepper
- 1 tsp salt
- ½ tsp cayenne pepper (optional, for heat)

Directions

1. Prepare the Marinade: In a bowl, mix together barbecue sauce, apple cider vinegar, olive oil, smoked paprika, garlic powder, onion powder, black pepper, salt, and cayenne pepper (if using).
2. Marinate the Turkey Legs: Place the turkey legs in a large resealable bag or dish, then pour the marinade over them. Seal the bag and marinate in the refrigerator for at least 1 hour (or up to 12 hours for more intense flavor).
3. Preheat the Pit Boss: Set your Pit Boss to 275°F and fill the hopper with pecan or hickory pellets. Preheat the grill for about 10 minutes.
4. Smoke the Turkey Legs: Remove the turkey legs from the marinade and place them directly on the grill. Smoke at 275°F for 2.5 to 3 hours, or until the internal temperature reaches 165°F, basting with any remaining marinade during the last 30 minutes of cooking.
5. Rest and Serve: Remove the turkey legs from the grill and let them rest for 10 minutes before serving. The turkey will be tender, juicy, and infused with a tangy BBQ flavor.

TIPS
- Add honey to the marinade or brush with extra barbecue sauce in the last 10 minutes for a sweeter flavor.
- Use pecan pellets for a subtle, nutty smoke or hickory for a more robust, traditional BBQ flavor.

Ingredients

- 1 lb ground beef (80/20 blend)
- 1 tsp kosher salt
- 1 tsp black pepper
- 4 slices cheddar cheese
- 4 brioche burger buns
- 1 tbsp butter (for toasting buns)
- Toppings (optional): lettuce, tomato, pickles, onions, ketchup, mustard, mayo

Serves

4

Prep Time

10 min

Cooking Time

30 min

SMOKED SMASH BURGERS

Directions

1. Preheat the Pit Boss Smoker: Set your Pit Boss to 225°F and load it with hickory pellets for a rich, smoky flavor that pairs well with beef.
2. Season the Beef: Divide the ground beef into 4 equal balls (about 4 oz each), season with salt and pepper, and avoid overworking the meat for a better smash burger texture.
3. Smoke the Patties: To infuse the meat with flavor, smoke the beef balls on the grill grates for 20 minutes at 225°F.
4. Crank Up the Heat: After smoking, remove the patties from the smoker and increase the temperature of the Pit Boss to 450°F for searing.
5. Smash the Burgers: Once the grill is hot, place each smoked beef ball on a cast iron skillet or flat plate and press down with a spatula to smash it into a thin patty. Hold for 10 seconds for a good sear.
6. Add Cheese: After flipping the burgers, top each patty with a slice of cheddar cheese and let it melt while the second side finishes cooking.
7. Toast the Buns: While the burgers are cooking, butter the inside of each brioche bun and toast them on the grill for about 30 seconds until golden brown.
8. Assemble the Smash Burgers: Place burger patty on a toasted bun, add toppings like lettuce, tomato, onions, or pickles, and finish with ketchup, mustard, or mayo.

TIPS

- Hickory pellets give the burgers a bold, smoky flavor that complements the beef perfectly.
- To make a juicier burger, blend diced bacon with ground beef before forming the patties.
- Ensure your grill is hot before smashing the patties to get that perfect crispy edge!

SMOKED PULLED BEEF

Prep time: 20 min	Cooking time: 8-10 hours	Serves: 6-8

Ingredients

- 4 lbs beef chuck roast
- 2 tbsp olive oil
- 1/4 cup kosher salt
- 2 tbsp black pepper
- 2 tbsp garlic powder
- 1 tbsp smoked paprika
- 1 tbsp onion powder
- 1 tsp cayenne pepper (optional)
- 1/2 cup beef broth
- 1/4 cup apple cider vinegar

Directions

1. Pat the beef chuck roast dry with paper towels. Rub the olive oil all over the meat to help the seasoning adhere.
2. Season the chuck roast with kosher salt, black pepper, garlic powder, smoked paprika, onion powder, and cayenne pepper (if using).
3. Set your Pit Boss Wood Pellet Grill to 225°F and use hickory or mesquite pellets.
4. Smoke the seasoned chuck roast at 225°F for 6-7 hours until the internal temperature reaches 160°F.
5. When the beef reaches 160°F, remove it from the smoker, place it in an aluminum baking dish, add beef broth and apple cider vinegar, cover tightly with aluminum foil, and return to the smoker.
6. Smoke for another 2-3 hours until the internal temperature reaches 200-205°F and the beef is fork-tender.
7. After removing the pan from the smoker, let the beef rest for 30 minutes to retain juices and make the meat easier to pull apart.
8. Using two forks, shred the beef into fine pieces, mixing it with the pan juices for extra flavor.
9. Serve the smoked pulled beef on its own, on sandwiches, or alongside your favorite barbecue sides.

TIPS

- Use hickory or mesquite pellets for a deep, smoky flavor that complements the rich, fatty beef.
- For extra flavor, add a splash of Worcestershire sauce or barbecue sauce to the meat before smoking.
- After pulling the beef, toss it back on the smoker at 375°F for 10-15 minutes to get crispy burnt ends.

REVERSE SEAR SMOKED TRI-TIP STEAK

Prep time: 10 min	Cooking time: 2 hours (including rest time)	Serves: 4

Ingredients

- 2.5-3 lbs tri-tip steak
- 2 tbsp olive oil
- 2 tbsp kosher salt
- 1 tbsp black pepper
- 1 tbsp garlic powder
- 1 tbsp onion powder
- 1 tsp smoked paprika
- 1/2 tsp cayenne pepper (optional)

Directions

1. Pat the tri-tip steak dry with paper towels. Rub olive oil all over the steak to help the seasoning stick.
2. Season the tri-tip generously with kosher salt, black pepper, garlic powder, onion powder, smoked paprika, and cayenne pepper (optional).
3. Set your Pit Boss Wood Pellet Grill to 225°F and use oak or hickory pellets for a robust, smoky flavor that complements beef well.
4. Remember to smoke the seasoned tri-tip at 225°F until the internal temperature reaches 115-120°F for medium-rare, which takes about 60-90 minutes. Use a meat thermometer to monitor the temperature.
5. After smoking, let the tri-tip rest for 15-20 minutes to redistribute juices and slightly increase the temperature.
6. While the steak rests, increase the smoker's temperature to 450-500°F or preheat a cast-iron skillet over high heat if using it for searing. Sear the tri-tip on each side for 2-3 minutes until a deep, flavorful crust forms.
7. Remember to let the seared tri-tip rest for 5 minutes before slicing. Slice against the grain for tenderness and serve promptly.

TIPS

- For a robust and earthy flavor that balances the richness of the tri-tip, use oak or hickory pellets.
- To add a layer of richness, you can melt butter over the steak after it's been grilled.
- Ensure you sear at a high temperature to create that perfect crispy, caramelized crust.
- The reverse sear method is excellent for thicker cuts of meat like tri-tip or ribeye.

Ingredients

- 3-4 lbs beef chuck roast
- 1 packet ranch seasoning mix (1 oz)
- 1 packet au jus gravy mix (1 oz)
- 1/4 cup unsalted butter, sliced
- 6-8 pepperoncini peppers
- 1/4 cup pepperoncini juice (from the jar)
- 1/2 cup beef broth
- 1 tbsp olive oil

Serves
6

Prep Time
15 min

Cooking Time
6-7 hours

SMOKED MISSISSIPPI POT ROAST

Directions

1. Prepare the Chuck Roast: Pat the chuck roast dry with paper towels and then rub olive oil to help the seasonings stick.
2. Season the Roast: Sprinkle ranch seasoning and au jus gravy mix evenly over the roast, pressing gently to ensure it adheres.
3. Preheat the Pit Boss Smoker: Set your Pit Boss Wood Pellet Grill to 250°F and use pecan or hickory pellets for a rich, sweet, smoky flavor that complements the tangy Mississippi roast.
4. Smoke the Roast: Place seasoned chuck roast on smoker grates. Smoke for 3-4 hours or until internal temperature reaches 160°F.
5. Add Butter, Peppers, and Broth: Once the roast reaches 160°F, transfer it to a large aluminum foil pan and add butter, pepperoncini peppers, juice, and beef broth.
6. Cover and Continue Smoking: Cover the pan tightly with aluminum foil and cook in the smoker at 250°F for 2-3 hours until the internal temperature reaches 200-205°F and the meat is tender.
7. Rest the Roast: After smoking, let the roast rest covered for 15-20 minutes before serving.
8. Shred and Serve: Shred the pot roast with two forks, mix with the pan juices, and serve with pepperoncini peppers for extra flavor.

TIPS

- Use pecan or hickory pellets for a balanced, smoky flavor that enhances the rich and tangy notes of the Mississippi roast.
- After shredding, put the pulled meat back on the smoker for 15 minutes at 375°F to create crisp edges.

GRILLED NASHVILLE HOT CHICKEN SANDWICH

Ingredients

- 4 boneless, skinless chicken thighs
- 1/4 cup hot sauce (such as Frank's RedHot)
- 1/4 cup buttermilk
- 2 tbsp olive oil
- 1 tbsp kosher salt
- 1 tbsp black pepper
- 1 tbsp garlic powder
- 1 tbsp smoked paprika
- 1 tsp cayenne pepper (adjust to taste)
- 4 brioche buns, toasted
- 1/2 cup dill pickles, sliced
- 1/4 cup mayonnaise
  For Nashville Hot Sauce
- 1/2 cup melted butter
- 1/4 cup cayenne pepper (adjust for heat)
- 1 tbsp brown sugar
- 1 tsp garlic powder
- 1 tsp smoked paprika
- 1/2 tsp chili powder

Directions

1. Mix hot sauce, buttermilk, olive oil, kosher salt, black pepper, garlic powder, smoked paprika, and cayenne pepper in a large bowl. Add the chicken thighs and toss to coat. Cover and marinate in the fridge for at least 1 hour or 24 hours for more flavor.
2. Set your Pit Boss Wood Pellet Grill to 375°F. Use hickory or cherrywood pellets for a smoky, slightly sweet flavor that complements the spicy chicken.
3. Remove the chicken from the marinade and shake off any excess. Place the chicken thighs directly on the grill grates and cook for 6-8 minutes per side until the internal temperature reaches 165°F.
4. While the chicken is grilling, make the hot sauce. Combine melted butter, cayenne pepper, brown sugar, garlic powder, smoked paprika, and chili powder in a small saucepan. Stir over low heat until well mixed. Keep warm.
5. Once the chicken is done, brush it generously with the Nashville hot sauce Spread mayonnaise on the toasted brioche buns, then layer the bottom buns with pickles. Place the grilled chicken thighs on the pickles and close with the top buns.
6. Serve the Nashville hot chicken sandwiches immediately with extra hot sauce on the side if desired.

TIPS
- Use hickory or cherrywood pellets for a bold, smoky flavor with a hint of sweetness that balances the chicken's heat.
- For a crispier texture and added crunch, grill the chicken thighs on high heat for a few minutes.

DOUBLE SMOKED HAM

Ingredients

- 8-10 lbs fully cooked, bone-in ham
- 1/2 cup Dijon mustard
- 1/2 cup brown sugar
- 1/4 cup honey
- 1/4 cup apple cider vinegar
- 1 tsp ground cinnamon
- 1 tsp ground cloves
- 1/2 tsp ground nutmeg
- 1/2 tsp ground black pepper

Directions

1. Set your Pit Boss Wood Pellet Grill to 225°F and use applewood or cherrywood pellets for a sweet, mild smoke that complements the natural flavor of the ham.
2. Remove packaging and netting from the fully cooked ham. On a cutting board, score the surface in a diamond pattern about 1/4-inch deep to help the glaze penetrate the meat.
3. Mix Dijon mustard, brown sugar, honey, apple cider vinegar, cinnamon, cloves, nutmeg, and black pepper in a saucepan over medium heat. Cook for about 5 minutes until well combined and slightly thickened. Set aside.
4. Smoke the ham at 225°F for 2-3 hours to absorb additional smoke flavor.
5. After 2-3 hours of smoking, brush the ham with glaze. Continue smoking for 1-2 hours, basting every 30 minutes.
6. Smoke the ham until the internal temperature reaches 140°F for juiciness.
7. After smoking, let the ham rest for 15-20 minutes before slicing to enhance flavor.

TIPS
- Use applewood or cherrywood pellets for a sweet, fruity smoke that perfectly matches the ham's natural saltiness.
- Add a bourbon or maple syrup splash to the glaze for a richer, more complex flavor.
- After glazing, increase the smoker's temperature to 275°F during the last 30 minutes to create a slightly crispy, caramelized crust.

Ingredients

- 3-4 lbs picanha roast (top sirloin cap, fat cap intact)
- 2 tbsp kosher salt
- 1 tbsp black pepper
- 1 tbsp garlic powder
- 1 tsp smoked paprika
- 1 tbsp olive oil

SMOKED BRAZILIAN PICANHA

Directions

1. Prepare the Picanha: Pat the picanha dry with paper towels and trim any excess silver skin or fat, but leave the thick fat cap intact for added flavor and moisture during smoking.
2. Score the Fat Cap: Score the fat cap in a crosshatch pattern without cutting into the meat to help seasoning and smoke penetrate intensely.
3. Season the Picanha: Rub olive oil over the roast, then grow generously with kosher salt, black pepper, garlic powder, and smoked paprika.
4. Preheat the Pit Boss Smoker: Set your Pit Boss Wood Pellet Grill to 250°F and use mesquite or oak pellets for a robust smoke that pairs well with picanha.
5. Smoke the Picanha: Remember to place the seasoned picanha on the smoker grates, fat cap side up, and smoke at 250°F for 2-3 hours until the internal temperature reaches 125°F for medium-rare or 135°F for medium. Use a meat thermometer to monitor the temperature closely.
6. Rest the Picanha: After reaching the desired temperature, remove the picanha from the smoker and let it rest for 10-15 minutes to redistribute the juices for a more tender and flavorful cut.
7. Sear the Picanha (Optional): For a crispy fat cap, sear the picanha over high heat on a grill or in a cast-iron skillet for 1-2 minutes on each side after resting.
8. Slice and Serve: Slice the picanha against the grain into thin strips. Serve as-is or with chimichurri sauce for an authentic Brazilian touch.

Serves

4-6

Prep Time

15 min

Cooking Time

2-3 hours

T I P S

- Use mesquite or oak pellets for a bold, earthy flavor that complements the beefy richness of picanha.
- Serve with chimichurri or a side of farofa (toasted cassava flour) for an authentic Brazilian experience.
- Finish the picanha under high heat on each side for a couple of minutes after smoking for an extra crispy fat cap.

SMOKED MEATLOAF

Prep time: 15 min

Cooking time: 2-3 hours

Serves: 6

Ingredients

- 2 lbs ground beef (80/20 blend)
- 1 lb ground pork
- 1 medium onion, finely chopped
- 2 garlic cloves, minced
- 1/2 cup breadcrumbs
- 2 large eggs
- 1/2 cup milk
- 1/4 cup ketchup
- 2 tbsp Worcestershire sauce
- 1 tbsp Dijon mustard
- 2 tsp kosher salt
- 1 tsp black pepper
- 1 tsp smoked paprika
- 1/2 tsp onion powder
- 1/2 tsp garlic powder
- 1/4 cup BBQ sauce (for glazing)

Directions

1. Combine ground beef, pork, onion, garlic, breadcrumbs, eggs, milk, ketchup, Worcestershire sauce, Dijon mustard, salt, pepper, smoked paprika, onion powder, and garlic powder in a mixing bowl. Mix gently
2. Form the mixture into a loaf on parchment paper or aluminum foil. Make sure it is compact and evenly shaped for even cooking.
3. Set your Pit Boss Wood Pellet Grill to 225°F.
4. Place the meatloaf directly on the smoker grates, ensuring it's supported by the parchment or foil. Smoke for about 2-2.5 hours until the internal temperature reaches 150°F.
5. Once the meatloaf reaches 150°F, brush the top with BBQ sauce for a sweet, tangy glaze. Increase the smoker's temperature to 275°F and cook for 30 minutes or until the internal temperature reaches 165°F.
6. Remove the meatloaf from the smoker and let it rest for 10 minutes before slicing. This will allow the juices to settle, ensuring a moist and flavorful meatloaf.

TIPS
- Use hickory or oak pellets for a deep, smoky flavor that enhances the boldness of the beef and pork mix.
- Add shredded cheddar cheese to the meat mixture or bacon strips on top for a richer flavor before smoking.
- Add another layer of BBQ sauce during the last 10 minutes of cooking for an extra-glossy finish.

SMOKED CARNE ASADA SKIRT STEAK TACOS

Prep time: 15 min
+ 2 h marinating time

Cooking time: 45 min

Serves: 4

Ingredients

- 2 lbs skirt steak
- 1/4 cup olive oil
- 1/4 cup fresh lime juice (about 2 limes)
- 1/4 cup orange juice (about 1 orange)
- 4 garlic cloves, minced
- 1 tbsp chili powder
- 1 tsp ground cumin
- 1 tsp smoked paprika
- 1 tsp oregano
- 1 tsp kosher salt
- 1/2 tsp black pepper
- 1/4 cup chopped fresh cilantro (optional for garnish)
- Corn tortillas (or carnivore-friendly cheese wraps)

Directions

1. Whisk together the olive oil, lime juice, orange juice, garlic, chili powder, cumin, smoked paprika, oregano, salt, and black pepper in a large bowl.
2. Marinate the skirt steak in the refrigerator for at least 2 hours or overnight for maximum flavor.
3. Preheat your Pit Boss Wood Pellet Grill to 225°F.
4. Remove the steak from the marinade and let any excess drip off. Place the steak directly on the smoker grates. Smoke the steak at 225°F for about 45 minutes or until the internal temperature reaches 125-130°F for medium-rare.
5. Once the steak has smoked, increase the grill temperature to 450°F. Sear the steak for 1-2 minutes on each side to create a nice crust.
6. Remove the steak from the grill and rest for 5-10 minutes. Then, slice it thinly against the grain for tender slices.
7. Warm the corn tortillas (or cheese wraps if following a low-carb diet) on the grill for about 30 seconds on each side. Assemble the tacos by filling each tortilla with slices of smoked carne asada. Garnish with fresh cilantro if desired.

TIPS
- Use mesquite pellets for a strong, earthy flavor that complements the marinade's citrus and spice.
- Add a chopped jalapeño to the marinade for a spicier kick, or sprinkle some crushed red pepper on the steak before smoking.
- Swap the corn tortillas for cheese wraps to make this a carnivore-friendly taco.

Ingredients

- 1 whole alligator (10-12 lbs, cleaned and skinned)
- 1/4 cup olive oil
- 1/4 cup Cajun seasoning
- 1 tbsp kosher salt
- 1 tbsp black pepper
- 2 tbsp garlic powder
- 1 tbsp paprika
- 1 tbsp onion powder
- 1 tbsp smoked paprika
- 1 tbsp dried thyme
- 1 lemon, sliced
- 1/2 cup melted butter
- 1/4 cup hot sauce (optional)

Serves

10-12

Prep Time

30 min

Cooking Time

5-6 hours

SMOKED WHOLE ALLIGATOR

Directions

1. Prepare the Alligator: Rinse the whole alligator and pat it dry with paper towels. Place it on a large cutting board or tray. Rub olive oil over the entire surface of the alligator to help the seasoning stick.
2. Season the Alligator: In a small bowl, mix together the Cajun seasoning, kosher salt, black pepper, garlic powder, paprika, onion powder, smoked paprika, and dried thyme. Generously rub the seasoning mixture over the entire alligator, covering the outside and the cavity.
3. Preheat the Pit Boss Smoker: Set your Pit Boss Wood Pellet Grill to 250°F.
4. Smoke the Alligator: Place the seasoned alligator directly on the smoker grates. Insert a meat thermometer into the thickest part of the tail to monitor the internal temperature. Smoke the alligator for 4-5 hours at 250°F.
5. Baste with Butter: Mix the melted butter with hot sauce (if using) in a small bowl. After the first hour of smoking, baste the alligator with the butter mixture every 45 minutes to moisten the meat and add flavor.
6. Monitor the Internal Temperature: Continue smoking the alligator until the internal temperature in the thickest part of the tail reaches 165°F. This should take around 5-6 hours.
7. Rest the Alligator: Once it reaches the desired temperature, remove it from the smoker and let it rest for 15-20 minutes.
8. Serve: Slice the alligator meat, starting with the tender tail. Serve with lemon slices on the side, and drizzle extra butter sauce if desired.

TIPS

- Use pecan or hickory pellets for a robust, smoky flavor that enhances alligator meat's lean texture and unique taste.
- If your alligator still has skin, crank the grill to 375°F during the last 20-30 minutes to crisp it up.

SMOKED BEEF TENDERLOIN WITH RED WINE REDUCTION

Prep time: 20 min **Cooking time: 2 hours** **Serves: 4-6**

Ingredients

- 2 lbs beef tenderloin
- 2 tbsp olive oil
- 2 tbsp kosher salt
- 1 tbsp black pepper
- 1 tbsp garlic powder
- 1 tsp dried rosemary
- 1 tsp dried thyme
  For the Red Wine Reduction
- 1 cup red wine (Cabernet Sauvignon or Merlot recommended)
- 1/2 cup beef broth
- 2 tbsp unsalted butter
- 2 cloves garlic, minced
- 1 small shallot, minced
- 1 tsp fresh thyme leaves (or 1/2 tsp dried thyme)
- 1 tbsp balsamic vinegar
- Salt and pepper, to taste

Directions

1. Pat the beef tenderloin dry with paper towels. Rub olive oil over the entire surface of the meat.
2. Combine kosher salt, black pepper, garlic powder, dried rosemary, and dried thyme in a small bowl. Gently rub the mixture over the tenderloin.
3. Set your Pit Boss Wood Pellet Grill to 225°F.
4. Smoke the beef tenderloin until it reaches an internal temperature of 125°F for medium-rare (1.5-2 hours). For medium, aim for an internal temperature of 135°F.
5. While the beef is smoking, prepare the red wine reduction. Melt butter in a saucepan, add minced garlic and shallots, and cook until softened (2-3 minutes).
6. Combine red wine, beef broth, thyme, and balsamic vinegar in a pot. Boil then simmer for 10-15 minutes until the sauce reduces by half. Season with salt and pepper. Keep warm until serving.
7. After reaching the desired temperature, remove the tenderloin from the smoker and let it rest for 10-15 minutes to allow the juices to redistribute.
8. Slice the smoked tenderloin into thick medallions and drizzle with red wine reduction. Serve with your favorite sides for an elegant meal.

TIPS
- Use oak or cherrywood pellets for a balanced smoke that complements the richness of the beef without overpowering the delicate flavors.
- If you prefer not to use red wine, substitute it with beef broth and balsamic vinegar for a flavorful reduction.
- After smoking, sear the tenderloin on high heat for 1-2 minutes per side to create a beautiful crust.

GRILLED CHICKEN THIGHS WITH SPICY MANGO GLAZE

Prep time: 15 min **Cooking time: 40 min** **Serves: 4**

Ingredients

- 8 bone-in, skin-on chicken thighs
- 2 tbsp olive oil
- 1 tbsp kosher salt
- 1 tbsp black pepper
- 1 tbsp smoked paprika
- 1 tsp garlic powder
- 1 tsp onion powder
  For the Spicy Mango Glaze
- 1 ripe mango, peeled and diced
- 1/4 cup honey
- 2 tbsp apple cider vinegar
- 1 tbsp soy sauce
- 1 tbsp hot sauce (or more to taste)
- 1 tsp red pepper flakes
- 1 tbsp lime juice

Directions

1. Pat the chicken thighs dry with paper towels. Rub them with olive oil, then season evenly with kosher salt, black pepper, smoked paprika, garlic powder, and onion powder. Set aside while preparing the glaze.
2. Combine the diced mango, honey, apple cider vinegar, soy sauce, hot sauce, red pepper flakes, and lime juice in a blender or food processor. Blend until smooth. Set aside.
3. Preheat your Pit Boss Wood Pellet Grill to 375°F.
4. Place the chicken thighs skin-side down on the grill grates. Grill for 20-25 minutes, flipping halfway through, until the internal temperature reaches 165°F. The skin should be crispy and golden.
5. In the last 10 minutes of cooking, brush the chicken thighs generously with the spicy mango glaze. Allow the glaze to caramelize slightly on the grill, flipping and brushing as needed to coat both sides.
6. Remove the chicken thighs from the grill and rest for 5 minutes. Serve with extra mango glaze on the side.

TIPS
- Use mesquite or hickory pellets for a robust and smoky flavor that pairs perfectly with the sweetness and spice of the mango glaze.
- If mango is out of season, substitute with pineapple for a tropical twist.
- Increase the hot sauce or add a pinch of cayenne pepper to the glaze for more spice.

Ingredients

- 8 pig wings (pork shanks)
- 2 tbsp olive oil
- 2 tbsp kosher salt
- 1 tbsp black pepper
- 1 tbsp smoked paprika
- 1 tbsp garlic powder
- 1 tsp onion powder
- 1 tsp cumin
- 1 tsp cayenne pepper (optional)
- 1/2 cup BBQ sauce (optional)

SMOKED PIG WINGS

Directions

1. Prepare the Pig Wings: Pat the pig wings dry with paper towels. Lightly coat them with olive oil to help the seasoning stick.
2. Season the Pig Wings: In a small bowl, combine kosher salt, black pepper, smoked paprika, garlic powder, onion powder, cumin, and cayenne pepper (if using). Rub the seasoning mixture all over the pig wings, ensuring they are evenly coated.
3. Preheat the Pit Boss Smoker: Set your Pit Boss Wood Pellet Grill to 250°F.
4. Smoke the Pig Wings: Place the seasoned pig wings directly on the smoker grates. Smoke for about 2-3 hours or until the internal temperature of the meat reaches 190°F. This ensures they are tender and juicy.
5. Optional BBQ Glaze: If you want a saucy finish, brush the pig wings with BBQ sauce during the last 20 minutes of cooking. Increase the heat to 300°F for a caramelized glaze.
6. Rest the Pig Wings: Once the pig wings are cooked, remove them from the smoker and let them rest for 10 minutes before serving.
7. Serve: Serve the pig wings as a main dish with your favorite sides or as a fun appetizer.

Serves
4

Prep Time
15 min

Cooking Time
2-3 hours

TIPS

- Applewood gives a sweet, mild flavor, while hickory adds a more potent, robust smoke—both are perfect for pork.
- Increase the smoker temperature to 400°F for the last 10-15 minutes of cooking for crispier skin.
- Marinate the pig wings overnight in apple cider vinegar, garlic, and Worcestershire sauce for extra flavor depth before smoking.

HICKORY AND OAK SMOKED BEEF JERKY

Ingredients

- 2 lbs beef top round or flank steak, thinly sliced (1/4-inch thick)
- 1/4 cup soy sauce
- 2 tbsp Worcestershire sauce
- 1 tbsp kosher salt
- 1 tbsp black pepper
- 1 tbsp garlic powder
- 1 tbsp onion powder
- 2 tsp smoked paprika
- 2 tbsp brown sugar (optional)
- 1 tsp red pepper flakes (optional, for heat)
- 1/2 tsp liquid smoke (optional for extra smokiness)

Directions

1. Thinly slice the beef into 1/4-inch strips, cutting against the grain for tender jerky. Place the slices in a large zip-top bag.
2. In a small bowl, whisk together soy sauce, Worcestershire sauce, kosher salt, black pepper, garlic powder, onion powder, smoked paprika, brown sugar, red pepper flakes (if using), and liquid smoke (optional).
3. Pour the marinade into the zip-top bag with the beef slices. Seal the bag, making sure the marinade evenly coats all the meat. Refrigerate for at least 6 hours or overnight for the best flavor.
4. Set your Pit Boss Wood Pellet Grill to 160°F.
5. Remove the beef from the marinade and pat dry with paper towels to remove excess moisture. Place the beef strips on the smoker grates, leaving space between each piece for proper airflow.
6. Smoke the beef at 160°F for 4-6 hours or until the jerky is dry but slightl pliable. Check for doneness by bending a piece—if it bends without breaking, the jerky is ready.
7. Once the jerky is done, please remove it from the smoker and let it cool completely. Store in an airtight container for up to 2 weeks if vacuum-sealed.

TIPS
- Use a mix of hickory and oak pellets for bold, smoky flavors. Hickory adds a rich smoke, while oak balances it with a milder, earthy note.
- Freeze the beef for 30 minutes before slicing to make cutting it into thin, uniform pieces easier.

SMOKED PORK BELLY

Ingredients

- 3 lbs pork belly, skin-on
- 2 tbsp olive oil
- 1/4 cup kosher salt
- 2 tbsp black pepper
- 1 tbsp smoked paprika
- 1 tbsp garlic powder
- 1 tbsp onion powder
- 1/2 tsp cayenne pepper (optional)
- 1/4 cup apple cider vinegar (for spritzing)

Directions

1. Pat the pork belly dry with paper towels. Score the skin in a crisscross pattern. Rub olive oil all over the pork belly, including the skin, to help the seasoning adhere.
2. Rub a seasoning blend of kosher salt, black pepper, smoked paprika, garlic powder, onion powder, and cayenne pepper (if using) all over the pork belly, including the skin.
3. Set your Pit Boss Wood Pellet Grill to 225°F.
4. Place seasoned pork belly on smoker grates, skin side up. Smoke at 225°F for 3-4 hours, spritzing with apple cider vinegar every hour.
5. Once the internal temperature of the pork belly reaches 190°F, increase the smoker's temperature to 375°F and continue cooking for 30-45 minutes until the skin becomes crispy and golden.
6. After smoking, let the pork belly rest for 15 minutes to redistribute juices and keep the meat tender.
7. Remember to slice the pork belly into thick pieces with crispy skin intact. Enjoy as a main dish or as part of a barbecue spread.

TIPS
- Use applewood or cherrywood pellets for a sweet, subtle smoke that enhances the natural flavor of the pork belly without overpowering it.
- Try brushing the pork belly with a maple syrup glaze during the last hour of smoking for a sweet, caramelized finish.
- If you want extra crispy skin, after smoking, pop the pork belly under the broiler in the oven for 3-5 minutes.

Ingredients

- 2 lbs sirloin steak, cut into 1-inch cubes
- 1/4 cup olive oil
- 1/4 cup soy sauce
- 2 tbsp Worcestershire sauce
- 2 tbsp red wine vinegar
- 2 tbsp lemon juice
- 2 tbsp honey
- 4 garlic cloves, minced
- 1 tsp black pepper
- 1 tsp smoked paprika
- 1 tsp onion powder
- 1/2 tsp dried oregano
- 1/2 tsp dried thyme
- Skewers (wooden or metal)

SMOKED MARINATED SIRLOIN KABOBS

Directions

1. Prepare the Marinade: In a medium bowl, whisk together olive oil, soy sauce, Worcestershire sauce, red wine vinegar, lemon juice, honey, minced garlic, black pepper, smoked paprika, onion powder, dried oregano, and dried thyme.
2. Marinate the Sirloin: Place the sirloin cubes into a large resealable plastic bag or container. Pour the marinade over the meat, seal, and refrigerate for 4-6 hours or overnight for best results.
3. Preheat the Pit Boss Smoker: Set your Pit Boss Wood Pellet Grill to 225°F.
4. Skewer the Meat: Remove the sirloin cubes from the marinade and discard the marinade. Thread the meat onto skewers, leaving space between each cube to ensure even cooking.
5. Smoke the Kabobs: Place the skewers directly on the smoker grates. Smoke the sirloin kabobs for about 45 minutes to 1 hour, or until the internal temperature reaches 135°F for medium-rare, or longer if desired.
6. Rest and Serve: Remove the kabobs from the smoker and let them rest for 5 minutes before serving. This helps the juices redistribute, keeping the meat tender and flavorful.

Serves

4

Prep Time

20 min

(+ 4-6 h marinating time)

Cooking Time

60 min

TIPS

- Mesquite or hickory pellets give the sirloin a bold, smoky flavor that pairs well with the marinade.
- Baste the kabobs with melted butter or reserved marinade for added moisture and flavor during the last 15 minutes of smoking.
- Consider adding bell peppers or onions to the skewers for a veggie option.

FISH AND SEAFOOD RECIPES

Ingredients

- 4 salmon fillets (about 6 oz each)
- 2 tbsp olive oil
- 1/4 cup Dijon mustard
- 1/4 cup honey
- 1 tbsp fresh lemon juice
- 1 tsp garlic powder
- 1 tsp smoked paprika
- 1/2 tsp black pepper
- 1/2 tsp kosher salt
- Lemon wedges for serving

SMOKED SALMON WITH HONEY-DIJON GLAZE

Directions

1. Prepare the Salmon: Pat the salmon fillets dry with paper towels and brush them lightly with olive oil to prevent sticking. Set aside.
2. Make the Honey-Dijon Glaze: In a small bowl, whisk together the Dijon mustard, honey, fresh lemon juice, garlic powder, smoked paprika, black pepper, and kosher salt until well combined.
3. Preheat the Pit Boss Smoker: Set your Pit Boss Wood Pellet Grill to 225°F.
4. Apply the Glaze: Brush the salmon fillets generously with the honey-Dijon glaze and coat them well on all sides.
5. Smoke the Salmon: Place the glazed salmon fillets on the smoker grates, skin side down. Close the lid and smoke for about 1.5 to 2 hours until the internal temperature reaches 145°F and the salmon flakes easily with a fork.
6. Baste During Smoking: Halfway through the smoking process, brush the salmon with more honey-Dijon glaze for an extra layer of flavor and moisture.
7. Serve: Once done, remove the salmon from the smoker and rest for 5 minutes. Serve with lemon wedges on the side for an extra citrusy kick.

Serves

4

Prep Time

15 min

Cooking Time

2 hours

TIPS

- Use applewood or alder pellets for a light, sweet smoke that enhances the salmon's natural flavors without overpowering them.
- Mix in 1 tsp soy sauce or balsamic vinegar into the glaze for a bolder taste.
- If you like a crispier skin, finish the salmon on the grill at 375°F for 5-7 minutes.

GRILLED SHRIMP SKEWERS WITH GARLIC LIME MARINADE

Prep time: 15 min
+ 30 min marinating time

Cooking time: 10 min

Serves: 4

Ingredients

- 1 lb large shrimp, peeled and deveined
- 3 tbsp olive oil
- 2 tbsp fresh lime juice (about 2 limes)
- 3 garlic cloves, minced
- 1 tsp kosher salt
- 1/2 tsp black pepper
- 1/2 tsp smoked paprika
- 1/4 tsp crushed red pepper flakes (optional)
- 2 tbsp fresh cilantro, chopped
- Lime wedges for serving
- Wooden or metal skewers (if using wooden, soak in water for 30 minutes prior)

Directions

1. In a medium bowl, whisk together olive oil, lime juice, minced garlic, kosher salt, black pepper, smoked paprika, and crushed red pepper flakes (if using).
2. Add the shrimp to the marinade, tossing to coat evenly. Cover and refrigerate for at least 30 minutes (but no longer than 1 hour) to let the flavors develop.
3. Preheat your Pit Boss Wood Pellet Grill to 400°F.
4. Thread the marinated shrimp onto the skewers, leaving a little space between each shrimp for even cooking.
5. Place the shrimp skewers directly on the grill grates. Grill for 2-3 minutes per side until the shrimp turn opaque and have a nice char. Avoid overcooking, as shrimp can become rubbery.
6. Remove the skewers from the grill and sprinkle with fresh cilantro. Serve with lime wedges on the side for an extra burst of citrus.

TIPS
- Cherrywood pellets add a subtle sweetness that complements the garlic-lime marinade, enhancing the shrimp's natural flavors.
- These shrimp skewers pair perfectly with grilled veggies or a fresh salad for a light and refreshing meal.

SMOKED SWORDFISH STEAKS WITH LEMON BUTTER

Prep time: 15 min

Cooking time: 60 min

Serves: 4

Ingredients

- 4 swordfish steaks (about 6 oz each)
- 2 tbsp olive oil
- 1 tsp kosher salt
- 1 tsp black pepper
- 1 tsp garlic powder
- 1/2 tsp smoked paprika
- 1/4 cup unsalted butter, melted
- 2 tbsp fresh lemon juice
- 1 tbsp fresh parsley, chopped
- Lemon wedges for serving

Directions

1. Pat the swordfish steaks dry with paper towels. Rub olive oil over both sides of the steaks to help the seasoning adhere.
2. Mix kosher salt, black pepper, garlic powder, and smoked paprika in a small bowl. Evenly season both sides of the swordfish steaks.
3. Set your Pit Boss Wood Pellet Grill to 225°F.
4. Place the seasoned swordfish steaks directly on the smoker grates. Smoke at 225°F for about 45 minutes to 1 hour or until the internal temperature reaches 130°F.
5. While the swordfish is smoking, melt the butter in a small saucepan over low heat. Stir in the fresh lemon juice and chopped parsley. Keep warm.
6. Once the swordfish reaches the desired temperature, please remove it from the smoker and rest for 5 minutes. Drizzle the warm lemon butter over each steak. Serve with lemon wedges on the side.

TIPS
- Use applewood or alderwood pellets for a mild, slightly fruity smoke that won't overpower the swordfish's natural flavor.
- Add a pinch of red pepper flakes to the lemon butter for a bit of heat, or sprinkle some freshly grated lemon zest over the steaks before serving for extra citrus brightness.
- Don'tSwordfish can dry out quickly, so make sure to pull it from the smoker as soon as it reaches 130°F for a perfectly moist texture.

Ingredients

For the Smoked Octopus

- 2 medium octopuses (about 2 lbs each, cleaned)
- 1/4 cup olive oil
- 3 garlic cloves, minced
- 1 lemon (zested and juiced)
- 1 tbsp smoked paprika
- 1 tsp dried oregano
- 1 tsp kosher salt
- 1/2 tsp black pepper
- 1/4 cup white wine
- 2 bay leaves

For the Chickpea Salad

- 1 can (15 oz) chickpeas, drained and rinsed
- 1/2 cup cherry tomatoes, halved
- 1/4 cup Kalamata olives, pitted and halved
- 1/4 cup red onion, finely sliced
- 1/4 cup cucumber, diced
- 2 tbsp fresh parsley, chopped
- 2 tbsp olive oil
- 1 tbsp red wine vinegar
- 1 tsp lemon juice
- Salt and pepper to taste

Serves

4

Prep Time

30 min

(+ 1h marinating time)

Cooking Time

2-3 hours

SMOKED OCTOPUS WITH MEDITERRANEAN CHICKPEA SALAD

Directions

1. Prepare the Octopus Marinade: In a bowl, combine olive oil, minced garlic, lemon zest, lemon juice, smoked paprika, oregano, salt, pepper, and white wine. Add bay leaves.
2. Marinate the Octopus: Place the cleaned octopuses in the marinade, coat well, cover, and refrigerate for at least 1 hour.
3. Preheat the Pit Boss Smoker: Set your Pit Boss Wood Pellet Grill to 225°F.
4. Smoke the Octopus: Remove the octopuses from the marinade, pat them dry, and place them directly on the smoker grates. Smoke at 225°F for 2-3 hours until tender and smoky-flavored, reaching an internal temperature of around 145°F.
5. Prepare the Mediterranean Chickpea Salad: While the octopus is smoking, prepare the salad. Combine chickpeas, cherry tomatoes, Kalamata olives, red onion, cucumber, and parsley in a large bowl. Whisk together olive oil, red wine vinegar, lemon juice, salt, and pepper in a small bowl. Pour the dressing over the salad and toss to coat. Set aside.
6. Finish and Serve: After smoking and tenderizing the octopus, cut the tentacles into bite-sized pieces and serve over Mediterranean chickpea salad. Drizzle with olive oil and lemon juice if desired.

TIPS

- Consider using cherrywood or applewood pellets for a mild smoke that enhances the delicate flavor of octopus.
- For a crispier exterior, sear the smoked octopus on a hot grill for 1-2 minutes per side after smoking.
- Add balsamic glaze or smoked sea salt to the dish to enhance the flavor.

SMOKED TILAPIA FILLETS

Ingredients

- 4 tilapia fillets (about 6-8 oz each)
- 2 tbsp olive oil
- 1 tbsp kosher salt
- 1 tsp black pepper
- 1 tsp garlic powder
- 1 tsp onion powder
- 1/2 tsp smoked paprika
- 1 lemon, sliced
- 1 tbsp fresh parsley, chopped (optional)

Directions

1. Rinse the tilapia fillets under cold water and pat them dry with paper towels. Rub each fillet with olive oil to help the seasoning adhere.
2. Combine the kosher salt, black pepper, garlic powder, onion powder, and smoked paprika in a small bowl. Sprinkle the seasoning evenly over both side of each fillet.
3. Set your Pit Boss Wood Pellet Grill to 225°F.
4. Place the seasoned tilapia fillets directly on the smoker grates. Close the lid and smoke at 225°F for about 45 minutes to 1 hour, or until the fish reaches an internal temperature of 145°F and flakes quickly with a fork.
5. Remove the tilapia from the smoker and transfer it to a serving platter. Garnish with fresh lemon slices and sprinkle with chopped parsley (if using) for a fresh, bright finish.

TIPS
- Use applewood or Alderwood pellets for a light, delicate smoke that enhances the tilapia's mild flavor without overpowering it.
- For a citrus twist, squeeze fresh lemon juice over the fillets during the last 10 minutes of smoking.

SMOKED HERB-CRUSTED HALIBUT

Ingredients

- 4 halibut fillets (6-8 oz each)
- 2 tbsp olive oil
- 1 tbsp kosher salt
- 1 tbsp black pepper
- 1 tbsp garlic powder
- 1 tsp lemon zest
- 1 tbsp fresh parsley, finely chopped
- 1 tbsp fresh dill, finely chopped
- 1 tbsp fresh thyme, finely chopped
- 2 tbsp butter, melted
- Lemon wedges for serving

Directions

1. Pat the halibut fillets dry with paper towels. Brush each fillet lightly with olive oil to help the seasoning stick.
2. Combine kosher salt, black pepper, garlic powder, and lemon zest in a small bowl. Rub this seasoning mixture evenly over each fillet.
3. In another bowl, mix the chopped parsley, dill, and thyme. Press the fresh herbs onto the top side of each fillet to create a flavorful crust.
4. Set your Pit Boss Wood Pellet Grill to 225°F.
5. Place the seasoned halibut fillets directly on the smoker grates. Smoke at 225°F for 45-60 minutes, or until the internal temperature reaches 130°F and the fish is flaky and tender.
6. In the last 10 minutes of smoking, brush the fillets with melted butter for added richness and flavor.
7. Remove the halibut from the smoker and serve immediately with lemon wedges for an extra citrus flavor.

TIPS
- Use alder or applewood pellets for a mild, sweet smoke that perfectly complements halibut's light flavor.
- For a brighter flavor, squeeze fresh lemon juice over the fillets before serving.
- For a crispier herb crust, increase the smoker temperature to 375°F during the last 5-10 minutes of cooking.

Ingredients

- 4 tuna steaks (about 6 oz each)
- 2 tbsp olive oil
- 1 tbsp soy sauce
- 1 tbsp sesame oil
- 1 tsp kosher salt
- 1 tsp black pepper
- 1/2 tsp garlic powder
- 1/2 tsp ginger powder
- 1/4 tsp cayenne pepper (optional)

Wasabi Mayo

- 1/2 cup mayonnaise
- 1 tbsp wasabi paste (adjust to taste)
- 1 tsp lemon juice
- 1/2 tsp soy sauce
- 1/2 tsp sesame oil

SMOKED TUNA STEAKS WITH WASABI MAYO

Directions

1. Prepare the Tuna Steaks: Pat the tuna steaks dry with paper towels. In a small bowl, whisk together the olive oil, soy sauce, sesame oil, kosher salt, black pepper, garlic powder, ginger powder, and cayenne pepper (if using). Rub the mixture evenly over both sides of the tuna steaks.
2. Preheat the Pit Boss Smoker: Set your Pit Boss Wood Pellet Grill to 225°F.
3. Smoke the Tuna Steaks: Put the tuna steaks on the smoker grates. Smoke for 45 minutes to 1 hour, or until the internal temperature reaches 130°F for medium-rare (adjust cooking time based on your preferred doneness).
4. Prepare the Wasabi Mayo: While the tuna is smoking, mix together the mayonnaise, wasabi paste, lemon juice, soy sauce, and sesame oil in a small bowl. Taste and adjust the wasabi level based on your preference for heat.
5. Rest and Serve: Once the tuna reaches your desired doneness, remove it from the smoker and rest for 5 minutes. Serve the tuna steaks with a generous dollop of wasabi mayo on the side or drizzled on top.

Serves
4

Prep Time
15 min

Cooking Time
60 min

TIPS

- Use alder or applewood pellets for a mild smoke that enhances the tuna without overpowering its flavor.
- After smoking, finish the tuna steaks on a high-heat grill for 1-2 minutes on each side for a crispy exterior.

SMOKED RAINBOW TROUT

Cooking time: 1-2 hours

Serves: 4

Ingredients

- 4 whole rainbow trout, cleaned (about 1 lb each)
- 1/4 cup kosher salt
- 1/4 cup brown sugar
- 4 cups water
- 1 lemon, sliced
- 2 tbsp olive oil
- 1 tbsp black pepper
- 1 tbsp garlic powder
- 1 tbsp dried dill
- 1/4 cup fresh parsley, chopped

Directions

1. In a large bowl, dissolve the kosher salt and brown sugar in water. Submerge the cleaned trout in the brine and refrigerate for 1-2 hours. This helps to season and keep the trout moist during smoking.
2. Set your Pit Boss Wood Pellet Grill to 180°F.
3. After brining, rinse the trout under cold water and pat dry with paper towels. Rub the olive oil over each trout. Sprinkle black pepper, garlic powder, and dried dill inside each fish's cavity. Add a few slices of lemon and some fresh parsley.
4. Place the trout directly on the smoker grates. Smoke the fish at 180°F for 1-2 hours or until the internal temperature reaches 145°F and the flesh is flaky and opaque.
5. Once the trout is fully cooked, remove it from the smoker and let it rest for 5 10 minutes before serving. The fish can be served whole or gently deboned for fillets.

TIPS
- Use Alderwood or applewood pellets for a delicate, slightly sweet smoke that enhances the trout's natural flavor without overpowering it.
- Brush the trout with lemon juice during the last 30 minutes of smoking for an extra burst of citrus.
- Increase the temperature to 350°F during the last 10 minutes of smoking for crispier trout skin.

SMOKED SALMON WITH AVOCADO-CILANTRO CREAM SAUCE

Prep time: 20 min

Cooking time: 1-2 hours

Serves: 4

Ingredients

- 4 salmon fillets (6 oz each)
- 2 tbsp olive oil
- 2 tsp kosher salt
- 1 tsp black pepper
- 1 tsp smoked paprika
- 1/2 tsp cumin
- 1 lime, sliced for garnish

For the Avocado-Cilantro Cream Sauce

- 1 ripe avocado
- 1/4 cup sour cream
- 1/4 cup fresh cilantro, chopped
- 1 tbsp fresh lime juice
- 1 garlic clove, minced
- Salt and pepper to taste
- 2 tbsp water (to thin, if necessary)

Directions

1. Rinse the salmon fillets and pat them dry with paper towels. Rub olive oil evenly over each fillet to help the seasoning stick.
2. In a small bowl, mix kosher salt, black pepper, smoked paprika, and cumin. Rub this mixture onto both sides of the salmon fillets.
3. Set your Pit Boss Wood Pellet Grill to 225°F.
4. Place the salmon fillets directly on the smoker grates, skin-side down. Smoke for 1 to 1.5 hours until the internal temperature reaches 145°F and the salmon flakes easily with a fork.
5. While the salmon is smoking, combine the avocado, sour cream, cilantro, lime juice, and minced garlic in a blender or food processor. Blend until smooth. If the sauce is too thick, add 1 tablespoon of water until it reaches the desired consistency. Season with salt and pepper to taste.
6. Once the salmon is finished, please remove it from the smoker and rest for a few minutes. Drizzle the avocado-cilantro cream sauce over the salmon fillets and garnish with fresh lime slices.

TIPS
- Use maple or pecan pellets for a subtle, sweet smoke that complements the creamy, tangy avocado sauce.
- For added heat, sprinkle chili powder or red pepper flakes into the sauce for a spicy kick.
- Add a little lime zest to the salmon's seasoning rub for an extra layer of citrusy brightness.

Ingredients

- 12 large sea scallops (about 1 lb)
- 12 slices of bacon
- 1 tbsp olive oil
- 1/2 tsp kosher salt
- 1/2 tsp black pepper
- 1/2 tsp garlic powder
- 1/2 tsp smoked paprika
- Toothpicks

BACON-WRAPPED SMOKED SCALLOPS

Directions

1. Preheat the Pit Boss Smoker: Set your Pit Boss Wood Pellet Grill to 225°F.
2. Prepare the Scallops: Pat the scallops dry with paper towels to remove excess moisture. This helps the bacon crisp up, and the scallops sear nicely. Drizzle the scallops with olive oil and sprinkle with kosher salt, black pepper, garlic powder, and smoked paprika.
3. Wrap the Scallops: Wrap each scallop with one slice of bacon and secure it with a toothpick. Ensure the bacon wraps tightly around the scallop but doesn't overlap too much so it cooks evenly.
4. Smoke the Scallops: Place the bacon-wrapped scallops directly on the smoker grates. Smoke for 45 minutes at 225°F or until the bacon is crispy and the scallops reach an internal temperature of 145°F.
5. Serve: Remove the scallops from the smoker and let them rest for a few minutes before serving. Serve them as an appetizer or alongside a main dish for a delicious, smoky treat.

Serves

4

Prep Time

15 min

Cooking Time

45 min

T I P S

- Use applewood or cherrywood pellets for a light, sweet smoke that enhances the delicate flavor of scallops and complements the savory bacon.
- For a tangy kick, brush the bacon with maple syrup or honey in the last 10 minutes of smoking.

SMOKED COD WITH CITRUS BRINE

Prep time: 15 min
(+ 2 h brining)

Cooking time: 1-2 hours

Serves: 4

Ingredients

- 4 cod fillets (6-8 oz each)
- 4 cups cold water
- 1/4 cup kosher salt
- 1/4 cup brown sugar
- 1 lemon, sliced
- 1 orange, sliced
- 1 lime, sliced
- 4 garlic cloves, crushed
- 1 tbsp black peppercorns
- 2 bay leaves
- 1 tbsp olive oil

Directions

1. Combine cold water, kosher salt, brown sugar, lemon, orange, lime slices, garlic cloves, black peppercorns, and bay leaves in a large bowl. Stir well until the salt and sugar dissolve completely.
2. Submerge the cod fillets in the brine, ensuring they are fully covered. Refrigerate for 2 hours. After brining, remove the fillets and pat them dry with paper towels.
3. Set your Pit Boss Wood Pellet Grill to 200°F.
4. Lightly brush the cod fillets with olive oil to prevent sticking. Place the fillets directly on the smoker grates, skin side down. Smoke the cod for 1 to 1.5 hours, or until the internal temperature reaches 145°F and the fish flakes easily with a fork.
5. Once the cod is fully cooked, remove it from the smoker and let it rest for a few minutes. For an extra burst of flavor, serve with fresh lemon slices or a light citrus sauce.

TIPS
- Use applewood or alderwood pellets for a subtle, sweet smoke that pairs perfectly with the delicate flavor of cod.
- For an extra burst of citrus, squeeze fresh lemon juice over the fillets right before serving.
- Increase the smoker temperature to 375°F for the last 10 minutes to achieve crispy skin on the cod.

SMOKED CRAB LEGS

Prep time: 10 min

Cooking time: 30 min

Serves: 4

Ingredients

- 2 lbs king or snow crab legs, thawed if frozen
- 1/4 cup unsalted butter, melted
- 2 tbsp olive oil
- 2 cloves garlic, minced
- 1 tbsp lemon juice
- 1/2 tsp smoked paprika
- 1/2 tsp kosher salt
- 1/4 tsp black pepper
- Lemon wedges (for serving)

Directions

1. Set your Pit Boss Wood Pellet Grill to 225°F.
2. Rinse the crab legs under cold water and pat them dry with paper towels. Lightly coat the crab legs with olive oil to prevent sticking during the smoking process.
3. Combine the melted butter, minced garlic, lemon juice, smoked paprika, kosher salt, and black pepper in a small bowl. Stir until well mixed.
4. Place the crab legs directly on the smoker grates. Smoke for 25-30 minutes, allowing the crab to absorb the smoky flavor.
5. About halfway through smoking, baste the crab legs with the garlic butter mixture. Continue to baste every 10 minutes until the crab is done.
6. Remove the crab legs from the smoker and brush with any remaining butter sauce. Serve immediately with lemon wedges on the side.

TIPS
- Applewood or cherrywood pellets provide a light, sweet smoke that won't overpower the delicate taste of crab.
- Serve the smoked crab legs with garlic butter dipping sauce for even more richness.

Ingredients

- 4 lobster tails (about 6-8 oz each)
- 1/4 cup unsalted butter, melted
- 2 tbsp olive oil
- Zest and juice of 1 lemon
- Zest and juice of 1 orange
- 2 cloves garlic, minced
- 1 tsp smoked paprika
- 1 tsp kosher salt
- 1/2 tsp black pepper
- Fresh parsley, chopped (for garnish)
- Fresh dill, chopped (for garnish)

Serves
4

Prep Time
15 min

Cooking Time
25-30 min

SMOKED LOBSTER TAILS WITH CITRUS BUTTER

Directions

1. Prepare the Lobster Tails: Using kitchen shears, carefully cut down the top shell of each lobster tail, stopping just before the tail fin. Gently pull the meat out of the shell, resting it on top of the shell without detaching it entirely.
2. Make the Citrus Butter: In a small bowl, mix together the melted butter, olive oil, lemon zest, lemon juice, orange zest, orange juice, minced garlic, smoked paprika, kosher salt, and black pepper.
3. Preheat the Pit Boss Smoker: Set your Pit Boss Wood Pellet Grill to 225°F.
4. Smoke the Lobster Tails: Brush the lobster meat generously with the citrus butter mixture, reserving some for basting. Place the lobster tails directly on the smoker grates, meat side up.
5. Cook Until Tender: Smoke the lobster tails for 25-30 minutes, basting with more citrus butter halfway through, until the meat is opaque and the internal temperature reaches 140°F.
6. Finish with Citrus Butter: Once cooked, remove the lobster tails from the smoker and drizzle any remaining citrus butter over the top.
7. Serve: Garnish with fresh parsley and dill for a bright finish. If desired, serve with extra lemon wedges on the side.

TIPS

- Use applewood or cherrywood pellets to impart a subtle, fruity smoke that complements the butter's citrus flavors.
- Serve the lobster tails with a light herb salad, mixing fresh dill, parsley, and chives with a drizzle of olive oil and lemon juice for a refreshing side.

SMOKED OYSTERS WITH GARLIC BUTTER

Prep time: 15 min　　　Cooking time: 30 min　　　Serves: 4

Ingredients

- 24 fresh oysters in the shell
- 1/2 cup unsalted butter, melted
- 4 garlic cloves, minced
- 2 tbsp fresh lemon juice
- 1 tbsp parsley, finely chopped
- 1/2 tsp smoked paprika
- 1/4 tsp black pepper
- 1/4 tsp sea salt
- Lemon wedges for serving

Directions

1. Clean the oyster shells under cold running water to remove dirt or debris. Then, preheat your Pit Boss Smoker to 225°F.
2. Melt the butter in a small saucepan over low heat. Add minced garlic, lemon juice, parsley, smoked paprika, black pepper, and sea salt. Stir well and set aside.
3. Carefully shuck the oysters, leaving the meat on the half shell. Discard the top shell and retain the bottom with the oyster meat inside.
4. Place the oysters in their half shells directly on the smoker grates. Smoke at 225°F for 25-30 minutes or until the oysters are plump and slightly firm to the touch.
5. After 15 minutes of smoking, brush the oysters generously with the garlic butter. Continue smoking for the remaining time.
6. Once the oysters are done, remove them from the smoker and serve immediately with additional garlic butter and lemon wedges on the side.

TIPS
- Use applewood or cherrywood pellets for a light, sweet smoke that complements the delicate flavor of oysters without overpowering them.
- Add a pinch of red pepper flakes to the garlic butter for a bit of heat, or top the oysters with a small sprinkle of grated Parmesan before the final basting.

SMOKED TUNA STEAKS WITH MANGO-HABANERO GLAZE

Prep time: 15 min　　　Cooking time: 1-2 hours　　　Serves: 4

Ingredients

- 4 fresh tuna steaks (6 oz each)
- 2 tbsp olive oil
- 1 tbsp kosher salt
- 1 tbsp black pepper
- 1 tsp smoked paprika
- 1 tsp ground cumin
- 1/2 tsp garlic powder
- 1/2 tsp onion powder
  For the Mango-Habanero Glaze
- 1 ripe mango, peeled and diced
- 1/4 cup honey
- 2 tbsp soy sauce
- 1 tbsp lime juice
- 1 habanero pepper, seeded and finely chopped (adjust for heat)
- 1 tsp fresh ginger, grated
- 1/4 cup water (or as needed for consistency)

Directions

1. Pat the tuna steaks dry with paper towels. Rub olive oil on both sides of each steak to help the seasoning adhere.
2. In a small bowl, mix kosher salt, black pepper, smoked paprika, ground cumin, garlic powder, and onion powder. Rub this seasoning blend evenly over both sides of the tuna steaks.
3. Set your Pit Boss Wood Pellet Grill to 225°F.
4. Place the tuna steaks directly on the smoker grates. Smoke at 225°F for about 1 to 1.5 hours or until the internal temperature reaches 125°F for medium-rare (adjust to your desired level of doneness).
5. While the tuna is smoking, prepare the glaze. Combine diced mango, honey, soy sauce, lime juice, habanero pepper, ginger, and water in a saucepan. Simmer over medium heat for 10-12 minutes until the mango has softened and the sauce has thickened. Blend until smooth.
6. In the last 15 minutes of smoking, brush the tuna steaks generously with the mango-habanero glaze to allow the flavors to set.
7. Once the tuna is cooked to your liking, remove it from the smoker. Let it rest for 5 minutes, then serve the steaks drizzled with more mango-habanero glaze on top.

TIPS
- Use applewood or alderwood pellets for a light, sweet smoke that enhances the flavor of tuna without overpowering its natural taste.
- If you prefer a milder glaze, reduce the habanero or substitute with a milder pepper like jalapeño.
- Serve the tuna steaks over a bed of coconut rice or grilled vegetables for a complete, exotic dish with an American twist.

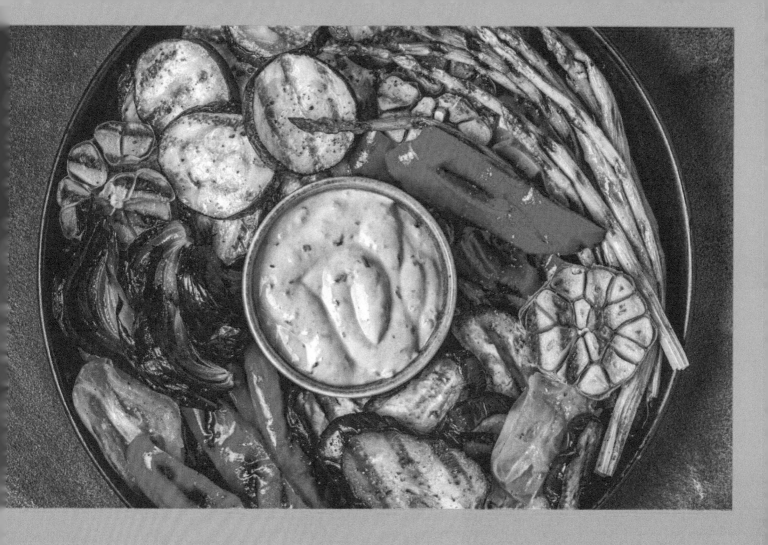

VEGAN AND VEGETARIAN RECIPES

Ingredients

For the Black Bean Burgers:

- 2 (15 oz) cans of black beans, drained and rinsed
- 1/2 cup breadcrumbs (use gluten-free if needed)
- 1/2 small red onion, finely diced
- 1/2 cup corn kernels (canned or frozen)
- 1/4 cup chopped fresh cilantro
- 2 garlic cloves, minced
- 1 tsp ground cumin
- 1 tsp smoked paprika
- 1/2 tsp chili powder
- 1/4 tsp black pepper
- 1 tbsp olive oil (for grilling)
- 4 burger buns (use vegan and gluten-free if needed)

For the Sweet Potato Wedges:

- 2 large sweet potatoes, cut into wedges
- 2 tbsp olive oil
- 1 tsp smoked paprika
- 1 tsp garlic powder
- 1/2 tsp black pepper
- 1/2 tsp kosher salt

Serves

4

Prep Time

20 min

Cooking Time

45 min

VEGAN SMOKED BLACK BEAN BURGERS WITH SMOKED SWEET POTATO WEDGES

Directions

For the Black Bean Burgers:

1. Mash the Beans: Mash the black beans in a bowl, leaving some texture for the burgers. They should be mostly mashed but not completely smooth.
2. Mix the Ingredients: Combine breadcrumbs, red onion, corn, cilantro, garlic, cumin, smoked paprika, chili powder, and black pepper with mashed beans. Mix well.
3. Form the Patties: Divide the mixture into 4 equal portions and form into patties. Add more breadcrumbs if the mixture feels too wet.
4. Preheat the Pit Boss Smoker: Set your Pit Boss to 350°F using applewood or hickory pellets.
5. Grill the Burgers: Brush the grill grates with olive oil to prevent sticking. Place the black bean patties on the smoker and cook for 6-8 minutes per side until they develop a good char and are heated through.

For the Smoked Sweet Potato Wedges:

1. Prepare the Sweet Potatoes: In a bowl, toss sweet potato wedges with olive oil, smoked paprika, garlic powder, black pepper, and salt.
2. Smoke the Sweet Potatoes: Smoke sweet potato wedges at 350°F for 30-35 minutes, turning halfway, until soft inside and crispy outside.
3. Serve: Toast the burger buns on the grill for 1-2 minutes, if desired. For a complete meal, serve the black bean burgers on the buns with your favorite vegan toppings and smoked sweet potato wedges on the side.

TIPS

- Use applewood or hickory pellets for a mild, balanced smokiness.
- For extra flavor, pair the burgers with a store-bought vegan BBQ sauce or a smoky vegan mayo.
- Add diced jalapeños or vegan cheese to the burgers for a spicier or creamier texture.

SMOKED MAC AND CHEESE

Prep time: 15 min **Cooking time: 1-2 hours** **Serves: 6-8**

Ingredients

- 1 lb elbow macaroni
- 4 tbsp unsalted butter
- 1/4 cup all-purpose flour
- 3 cups whole milk
- 1 cup heavy cream
- 4 cups shredded sharp cheddar cheese
- 2 cups shredded gouda cheese (or another smoky cheese)
- 1 tsp mustard powder
- 1 tsp garlic powder
- 1 tsp onion powder
- 1/2 tsp smoked paprika
- Salt and pepper to taste
- 1/2 cup panko breadcrumbs (optional for topping)

Directions

1. Pre-cook the elbow macaroni according to the package directions until al dente. Drain and set aside.
2. Melt butter in a saucepan, whisk in flour, then gradually add milk and cream until thickened.
3. Remove the saucepan from heat and stir in the cheddar and gouda cheeses until fully melted and smooth. Add mustard powder, garlic powder, onion powder, smoked paprika, and season with salt and pepper to taste.
4. Pour the cooked macaroni into a large mixing bowl, and add the cheese sauce. Stir to coat the pasta evenly.
5. Preheat your Pit Boss Wood Pellet Grill to 225°F. Use hickory or cherrywood pellets.
6. Pour mac and cheese into a greased pan and sprinkle with panko for a crispy finish.
7. Smoke the mac and cheese for 1.5 to 2 hours until golden brown and bubbling.
8. Let the mac and cheese rest for 5-10 minutes after removing it from the smoker before serving to allow it to firm up slightly.

TIPS
- Use hickory or cherrywood pellets for a smoky, subtle flavor to complement the rich cheeses without overpowering them.
- Add cooked bacon bits or smoked sausage slices to the mac and cheese before smoking for an extra savory twist.
- After smoking the mac and cheese, broil it in the oven for 2-3 minutes for a crispier top.

SMOKED BALSAMIC PORTOBELLO MUSHROOMS

Prep time: 10 min **Cooking time: 60 min** **Serves: 4**

Ingredients

- 4 large portobello mushrooms, stems removed
- 1/4 cup balsamic vinegar
- 2 tbsp olive oil
- 2 garlic cloves, minced
- 1 tbsp soy sauce
- 1 tsp dried thyme
- 1/2 tsp black pepper
- 1/4 tsp salt

Directions

1. Wipe the portobello mushrooms with a damp paper towel to clean them. Remove the stems and set the mushrooms aside.
2. Whisk together the balsamic vinegar, olive oil, minced garlic, soy sauce, dried thyme, black pepper, and salt in a small bowl.
3. Place the portobello mushrooms in a shallow dish and pour the balsamic marinade. Let them marinate for 15-30 minutes, flipping halfway through to ensure they absorb the flavors evenly.
4. Set your Pit Boss Wood Pellet Grill to 225°F. Use maple or applewood pellets for a mild, sweet smoke that complements the mushrooms' earthiness.
5. Place the marinated mushrooms directly on the smoker grates, gill side up. Smoke for 45 minutes to 1 hour until the mushrooms are tender and have absorbed the smoky flavor.
6. Remove the smoked portobello mushrooms from the smoker and let them rest for a few minutes before serving. Slice and enjoy as a side dish, or use them as a meat substitute for burgers or sandwiches.

TIPS
- For a subtle, sweet-smoke flavor, use maple or applewood pellets to enhance the natural flavors of the mushrooms without overshadowing them.
- For extra depth, sprinkle some grated Parmesan cheese or drizzle with a balsamic reduction before serving.
- These mushrooms can be sliced and used in salads, as a main dish, or as a vegetarian-friendly burger patty.

Ingredients

- 2 (8 oz) blocks of Philadelphia cream cheese
- 2 tbsp olive oil
- 1 tsp smoked paprika
- 1 tsp garlic powder
- 1 tsp onion powder
- 1/2 tsp black pepper
- 1/4 tsp cayenne pepper (optional)
- 1 tbsp fresh chives, chopped (optional, for garnish)

SMOKED PHILADELPHIA CREAM CHEESE

Directions

1. Prepare the Cream Cheese: Place the cream cheese blocks on a small wire rack or directly on a baking sheet lined with parchment paper. Using a sharp knife, score the top of each cream cheese block in a crosshatch pattern to allow for even smoking and seasoning absorption.
2. Season the Cream Cheese: Rub each cheese block with olive oil to help the seasonings stick. Mix smoked paprika, garlic powder, onion powder, black pepper, and cayenne pepper (if using). Sprinkle the seasoning blend generously over the cream cheese's top sides.
3. Preheat the Pit Boss Smoker: Set your Pit Boss Wood Pellet Grill to 200°F. Use applewood or pecan pellets.
4. Smoke the Cream Cheese: Place the cream cheese on the smoker grates (or on the rack if using). Smoke for 2 hours until it becomes golden in color and has a slightly firm outer texture.
5. Serve: Once smoked, remove the cream cheese from the smoker and let it cool for a few minutes. Garnish with fresh chopped chives (optional) and serve with crackers, vegetables, or as a spread for sandwiches and bagels.

Serves
6-8

Prep Time
5 min

Cooking Time
2 hours

T I P S

- Use applewood or pecan pellets for a light, sweet smoke that enhances the cream cheese's flavor without overpowering it.
- Mix some chopped jalapeños or crushed red pepper flakes into the seasoning for a spicier version.

SMOKED STUFFED BELL PEPPERS

Prep time: 20 min　　**Cooking time: 2 hours**　　**Serves: 4**

Ingredients

- 4 large bell peppers (any color)
- 1 cup cooked quinoa
- 1 can (15 oz) black beans, drained and rinsed
- 1 cup corn kernels (fresh or frozen)
- 1/2 cup diced tomatoes (fresh or canned, drained)
- 1 small onion, finely chopped
- 2 cloves garlic, minced
- 1 tbsp olive oil
- 1 tbsp chili powder
- 1 tsp cumin
- 1 tsp smoked paprika
- 1/2 tsp salt
- 1/4 tsp black pepper
- 1 cup vegan shredded cheese (optional)
- 2 tbsp fresh cilantro, chopped (for garnish)

Directions

1. Slice off the tops of the bell peppers and remove the seeds and membranes. Set the peppers aside.
2. Heat olive oil in a skillet over medium heat. Add the onion and garlic, sautéing until softened (about 5 minutes). Add the cooked quinoa, black beans, corn, diced tomatoes, chili powder, cumin, smoked paprika, salt, and black pepper. Stir until everything is combined and heated through, about 5 minutes.
3. Spoon the quinoa and bean mixture into each bell pepper, packing it tightly. Sprinkle some vegan shredded cheese on top if using.
4. Set your Pit Boss Wood Pellet Grill to 250°F. Use applewood or cherrywood pellets.
5. Place the stuffed peppers on the smoker grates and smoke for about 1.5 to 2 hours, or until the peppers are tender and the filling is heated through. If using vegan cheese, let it melt during the last 15 minutes of smoking.
6. Remove the peppers from the smoker, garnish with fresh cilantro, and let them cool for a few minutes before serving.

TIPS
- Applewood or cherrywood pellets bring a light, fruity smoke that pairs beautifully with the vegetables.
- Mix in cooked lentils or crumbled tofu into the filling for extra plant-based protein.
- Add diced jalapeños or a dash of hot sauce for a spicy kick.

SMOKED CHICKPEA AND SWEET POTATO BURGERS

Prep time: 20 min　　**Cooking time: 60 min**　　**Serves: 4**

Ingredients

- 1 large sweet potato (about 1 lb)
- 1 can (15 oz) chickpeas, drained and rinsed
- 1/2 cup breadcrumbs (use gluten-free if needed)
- 1/4 cup red onion, finely diced
- 2 cloves garlic, minced
- 1 tbsp olive oil
- 1 tsp smoked paprika
- 1 tsp cumin
- 1/2 tsp ground coriander
- Salt and pepper, to taste
- 1 tbsp fresh parsley, chopped
- 1 tbsp lemon juice
- Olive oil spray or additional olive oil for grilling

Directions

1. Set your Pit Boss Wood Pellet Grill to 225°F. For this vegetarian dish, use applewood or alderwood pellets.
2. Smoke the sweet potato for 45-50 minutes until tender, then let it cool.
3. Mash the drained chickpeas and smoked sweet potato together until well combined.
4. Mix breadcrumbs, red onion, garlic, olive oil, smoked paprika, cumin, coriander, salt, pepper, parsley, and lemon juice. Combine until cohesive.
5. Divide the mixture into four equal portions and shape them into burger patties. If the mixture is too sticky, add more breadcrumbs until it's easier to handle.
6. Spray or brush burger patties with olive oil. Smoke at 225°F for 15-20 minutes for a mild smoky flavor.
7. After smoking, increase the Pit Boss temperature to 375°F. Grill the patties for about 3-4 minutes per side until they develop a crispy exterior and are heated through.
8. Serve the smoked chickpea and sweet potato burgers on your favorite buns with toppings like lettuce, tomato, avocado, and vegan mayo.

TIPS
- Applewood or Alderwood pellets are ideal for this recipe because they provide a mild, sweet smoke that pairs well with the natural sweetness of sweet potato and chickpeas.
- You can add your favorite spices or herbs to the burger mix, such as fresh cilantro or a pinch of smoked chipotle powder for some heat.
- Use gluten-free breadcrumbs if needed, and serve on gluten-free buns.

Ingredients

- 2 tbsp olive oil
- 1 large onion, diced
- 3 garlic cloves, minced
- 1 red bell pepper, diced
- 1 yellow bell pepper, diced
- 2 cans (15 oz each) black beans, drained and rinsed
- 1 can (15 oz) kidney beans, drained and rinsed
- 1 can (15 oz) diced tomatoes
- 1 can (6 oz) tomato paste
- 1 cup vegetable broth
- 2 tbsp chili powder
- 1 tbsp smoked paprika
- 1 tsp cumin
- 1 tsp ground coriander
- 1 tsp dried oregano
- 1/2 tsp cayenne pepper (optional)
- Salt and pepper to taste
- 1 cup corn kernels (fresh or frozen)
- 1 tbsp soy sauce (optional for umami)
- 1 tbsp apple cider vinegar (optional for acidity)
- 1/4 cup fresh cilantro, chopped (optional for garnish)

Serves

6-8

Prep Time

20 min

Cooking Time

2-3 hours

SMOKED VEGAN CHILI

Directions

1. Preheat the Pit Boss Smoker: Set your Pit Boss Wood Pellet Grill to 225°F. Use hickory or mesquite pellets.
2. Prepare the Base: Heat the olive oil in a cast iron Dutch oven or heavy-duty, smoker-safe pot. Add the diced onion and garlic, sauté until soft and translucent, for about 5 minutes.
3. Add the Peppers: Stir in the red and yellow bell peppers, cooking for another 5 minutes until softened.
4. Add Spices and Seasoning: Mix in the chili powder, smoked paprika, cumin, ground coriander, oregano, and cayenne pepper (if using). Stir for 1 minute to let the spices bloom and become fragrant.
5. Add Beans and Tomatoes: Add the black beans, kidney beans, diced tomatoes, tomato paste, and vegetable broth to the pot. Stir well to combine all the ingredients.
6. Transfer to the Pit Boss Smoker: Cover the Dutch oven or pot with the smoker grates to allow the chili to absorb the smoke. Smoke the chili at 225°F for 1.5-2 hours, stirring occasionally to ensure it doesn't stick to the bottom.
7. Add Corn and Adjust Seasoning: After 1.5-2 hours, stir in the corn kernels and soy sauce (if using). Let the chili continue to smoke for 20-30 minutes to absorb even smoky flavor. Taste and adjust seasoning with salt, pepper, and apple cider vinegar for brightness.
8. Serve: Remove the chili from the smoker once it is thick and flavorful. Serve hot, garnished with fresh cilantro if desired. Enjoy with smoked tortilla chips or your favorite vegan toppings.

TIPS

- Use hickory for robust smoke, mesquite for an intense, earthy flavor, or applewood for a subtle sweetness.
- For extra heartiness, you can add diced zucchini, mushrooms, or carrots to the chili before smoking.
- Add a chopped jalapeño or extra cayenne pepper if you like spicy chili.

PIZZA AND BREAD RECIPES

Ingredients

- 1 lb pizza dough (store-bought or homemade)
- 1 large boneless, skinless chicken breast
- 1 cup BBQ sauce (divided)
- 1 cup shredded mozzarella cheese
- 1/2 cup shredded cheddar cheese
- 1/4 cup red onion, thinly sliced
- 1/4 cup fresh cilantro, chopped (optional)
- 1 tbsp olive oil
- 1 tsp garlic powder
- Salt and pepper to taste
- 1/2 tsp smoked paprika

Serves

4

Prep Time

20 min

(+ 1 hour for dough rising if making from scratch)

Cooking Time

45-60 min

SMOKED BBQ CHICKEN PIZZA

Directions

1. Preheat the Pit Boss Smoker: Set your Pit Boss to 250°F. Use applewood or cherrywood pellets.
2. Prepare the Chicken: Rub the chicken breast with olive oil, salt, pepper, garlic powder, and smoked paprika. Smoke at 250°F for about 45 minutes or until the internal temperature reaches 165°F. Remove, shred, and toss with 1/4 cup of BBQ sauce.
3. Preheat for Pizza Cooking: Increase the temperature of the Pit Boss to 400°F for cooking the pizza. If using a pizza stone, place it in the smoker to preheat.
4. Prepare the Dough: When using store-bought dough, follow the package instructions. If making dough from scratch, roll it to your desired thickness on a lightly floured surface and transfer it to a pizza peel or a baking sheet dusted with flour or cornmeal for easy transfer.
5. Assemble the Pizza: Spread BBQ sauce on pizza dough, add shredded chicken, mozzarella and cheddar cheese, and sliced red onions.
6. Smoke the Pizza: Transfer the assembled pizza to the preheated pizza stone or smoker grates. Close the lid and smoke the pizza at 400°F for 15-20 minutes, until the crust is golden and crispy and the cheese is bubbly and melted.
7. Finish and Serve: Sprinkle the pizza with fresh chopped cilantro (optional) after smoking. Let it cool before slicing and serving.

TIPS

- Use applewood or cherrywood pellets for a mild, sweet smoke that enhances BBQ sauce without overpowering pizza. Hickory pellets are a good choice if you prefer a deeper smoke flavor.
- For an extra crispy crust, brush the edges of the pizza dough with olive oil before placing it in the smoker.

SMOKED PEPPERONI PIZZA

Prep time: 15 min
(+ 1 h for dough rising)

Cooking time: 15-20 min

Serves: 4

Ingredients

For the Dough:
- 2 1/4 tsp active dry yeast (1 packet)
- 1 tsp sugar
- 1 1/2 cups warm water (110°F)
- 3 1/2 cups all-purpose flour
- 2 tbsp olive oil
- 1 tsp kosher salt

For the Toppings:
- 1 cup pizza sauce
- 2 cups shredded mozzarella cheese
- 30-40 slices of pepperoni
- 1/4 cup grated Parmesan cheese
- 1 tbsp olive oil (for brushing crust)
- 1 tsp dried oregano
- 1 tsp crushed red pepper flakes (optional)

Directions

1. Mix warm water, sugar, and yeast. Let it sit for 5-10 minutes until foamy. In a separate bowl, combine flour, salt, and olive oil. Add the yeast mixture and stir to form a dough.
2. Knead the dough on a lightly floured surface for 5-7 minutes until smooth and elastic. Place the dough in a greased bowl, cover, and let it rise warmly for 1 hour or until doubled in size.
3. Set your Pit Boss Wood Pellet Grill to 425°F. Use mesquite or oak pellets.
4. Punch down the dough and divide it into two equal portions. Roll each portion into a 12-inch circle on a lightly floured surface.
5. Spread pizza sauce on rolled-out dough, leaving a 1-inch border. Add mozzarella, pepperoni, Parmesan, and oregano.
6. Place the pizza stone or pan on the smoker grates and smoke the pizza at 425°F for 15-20 minutes. Rotate the pizza halfway through cooking for even browning.
7. Once the pizza is cooked, remove it from the smoker and let it cool for a few minutes. Slice and enjoy your smoked pepperoni pizza!

TIPS
- Use mesquite or oak pellets for a bold, smoky flavor that pairs well with the pepperoni and cheese.
- Add other toppings like mushrooms, onions, or olives for extra flavor.
- Place the pizza directly on the grill grates for the last 5 minutes of cooking. For an extra crispy crust

SMOKED CHEDDAR JALAPEÑO BREAD

Prep time: 20 min
(+ 1 h for dough rising)

Cooking time: 45-50 min

Serves: 6-8

Ingredients

- 3 cups all-purpose flour
- 1 packet (2 1/4 tsp) active dry yeast
- 1 cup warm water (about 110°F)
- 1 tbsp sugar
- 1 tsp salt
- 1 1/2 cups sharp cheddar cheese, shredded
- 2-3 fresh jalapeños, diced (remove seeds for less heat)
- 1/4 cup unsalted butter, melted
- 1/4 cup milk (for brushing)

Directions

1. In a small bowl, combine warm water, sugar, and yeast. Stir gently and let it sit for 5-10 minutes until it becomes frothy.
2. Combine flour, salt, activated yeast, and melted butter in a bowl. Stir into a dough.
3. Fold in the shredded cheddar cheese and diced jalapeños. Mix until the ingredients are evenly distributed throughout the dough.
4. Knead the dough on a floured surface for 5-7 minutes until smooth and elastic. Add more flour if sticky; let it rise for about 1 hour until doubled in size.
5. While the dough is rising, preheat your Pit Boss Wood Pellet Grill to 350°F. Use applewood or maple pellets.
6. Once the dough has risen, punch it down and shape it into a loaf or divide it into smaller rolls, depending on your preference.
7. Remember to brush the shaped dough with milk, place it on a greased baking sheet, and bake in the smoker for 45-50 minutes until the internal temperature reaches 190°F and the crust is golden brown.
8. Remove the bread from the smoker and let it cool for 10-15 minutes before slicing. Serve warm for the best flavor.

TIPS
- Use applewood or maple pellets for a subtle smoky sweetness that balances the cheddar and jalapeño flavors.
- For a spicier kick, leave the seeds in the jalapeños or add a pinch of cayenne pepper to the dough.
- Sprinkle a bit of extra cheddar on top of the loaf before baking for a cheesy, golden crust.

DESSERT RECIPES

Ingredients

- 1 (9-inch) unbaked pie crust (homemade or store-bought)
- 1 can (15 oz) pumpkin puree
- 1 cup heavy cream
- 1/2 cup brown sugar, packed
- 1/4 cup granulated sugar
- 2 large eggs
- 1 tsp ground cinnamon
- 1/2 tsp ground ginger
- 1/4 tsp ground cloves
- 1/4 tsp ground nutmeg
- 1/2 tsp salt
- 1 tsp vanilla extract

SMOKED PUMPKIN PIE

Directions

1. Prepare the Pit Boss Smoker: Preheat your Pit Boss Wood Pellet Grill to 350°F using pecan or maple pellets.
2. Prepare the Pie Crust: Roll out your unbaked pie crust and press it into a 9-inch pie pan. Crimp the edges as desired and set aside while preparing the filling.
3. Make the Pumpkin Filling: In a large mixing bowl, whisk together the pumpkin puree, heavy cream, brown sugar, granulated sugar, eggs, cinnamon, ginger, cloves, nutmeg, salt, and vanilla extract. Mix until smooth and well combined.
4. Fill the Crust: Pour the pumpkin filling into the prepared pie crust, smoothing the top with a spatula to ensure it's even.
5. Smoke the Pumpkin Pie: Place the pie on the smoker and cook for 1 to 1 hour and 15 minutes, or until the filling is set but still slightly jiggly in the center. You can check the internal temperature, which should read about 175°F when done.
6. Cool the Pie: Remove the pumpkin pie from the smoker and let it cool completely at room temperature for at least 2 hours before serving. This allows the filling to be fully set.
7. Serve: Slice and serve your smoked pumpkin pie with a whipped or vanilla ice cream dollop.

Serves

8

Prep Time

20 min

Cooking Time

1 h 15 min

TIPS

- Pecan or maple pellets give the pie a subtle, nutty sweetness that pairs beautifully with the spiced pumpkin filling.
- If the crust edges brown too quickly, cover them with foil halfway through cooking to prevent over-browning.

SMOKED APPLE PIE

Cooking time: 1h 15 min

Serves: 8

Ingredients

- 2 pie crusts (homemade or store-bought, for a 9-inch pie)
- 6-7 medium Granny Smith apples, peeled, cored, and sliced
- 1 tbsp lemon juice
- 3/4 cup granulated sugar
- 1/4 cup brown sugar, packed
- 1 tsp ground cinnamon
- 1/4 tsp ground nutmeg
- 1/4 tsp ground allspice
- 2 tbsp all-purpose flour
- 2 tbsp unsalted butter, cut into small pieces
- 1 egg (beaten, for brushing)
- 1 tbsp granulated sugar (for sprinkling on top)

Directions

1. Preheat your Pit Boss Wood Pellet Grill to 350°F using applewood or pecan pellets.
2. Toss sliced apples with lemon juice, sugars, spices, and flour until well coated.
3. Roll out the pie crust and place it in a 9-inch pie pan. Pour in apple mixture and dot with butter.
4. Roll out the second pie crust and lay it over the apples. Trim any excess dough and crimp the edges together to seal. Cut a few small slits in the top crust to allow steam to escape.
5. Brush the top crust with the beaten egg and sprinkle with granulated sugar for a golden, shiny finish.
6. Place the pie on the smoker and cook for about 1 to 1 hour and 15 minutes, until the crust is golden brown and the apple filling is bubbly. You can check if the apples are tender by inserting a knife into the center.
7. Remove the pie from the smoker and let it cool for 1-2 hours before serving to allow the filling to set.
8. Slice the smoked apple pie and serve it with vanilla ice cream or whipped cream for a perfect pairing.

TIPS
- Use applewood or pecan pellets to enhance the fruity sweetness of the apples while adding a subtle smoky depth to the pie.
- Add a handful of raisins or chopped nuts to the apple mixture for texture and flavor.
- If the edges of the pie start to brown too quickly, cover them with aluminum foil halfway through baking.

MODERN DONUT S'MORE

Prep time: 15 min

Cooking time: 10 min

Serves: 4

Ingredients

- 4 plain donuts (glazed or unglazed, your choice)
- 4 large marshmallows
- 4 squares of dark chocolate (about 1 oz each)
- 2 tbsp crushed graham crackers
- 1 tbsp unsalted butter, melted
- 1/4 tsp sea salt (optional)

Directions

1. If you're using your Pit Boss or any grill, preheat it to medium heat, around 350°F. You can use indirect heat for a more controlled toasting process or direct heat for quicker grilling.
2. Skewer the marshmallows and place them over the heat, rotating until they turn golden brown and slightly charred on all sides. This should take about 2-3 minutes. Once toasted, set aside.
3. For unglazed donuts, brush with melted butter. Place on the grill for 1-2 minutes per side to warm and create a slight crisp.
4. In a small bowl, melt the chocolate squares in the microwave for 30-second intervals, stirring until smooth.
5. Slice each donut in half like a bagel. Spread melted chocolate on the bottom half of each donut. Place a toasted marshmallow on top of the chocolate, sprinkle crushed graham crackers over the marshmallow, then top with the other half of the donut.
6. For an elevated twist, drizzle extra melted chocolate over the top of the assembled s'mores and sprinkle lightly seasoned salt.
7. Serve the donut s'mores immediately, while ws'mores are gooey for the best taste and texture.

TIPS
- Try using flavored donuts, such as chocolate or cinnamon sugar, for a unique twist on the traditional s'more.
- For example, mix the crushed graham crackers with toasted nuts like almonds or pecans.
- Toast the marshmallows without toasting the marshmallow,ws; use a light d to give them a subtle smoky flavor that pairs well with the chocolate and donuts.

SMOKED PEACH COBBLER

Prep time: 20 min   **Cooking time: 60 min**   **Serves: 6-8**

Ingredients

- 6 ripe peaches, sliced (about 5 cups)
- 1/2 cup granulated sugar
- 1/4 cup brown sugar
- 1 tsp cinnamon
- 1/4 tsp nutmeg
- 1 tbsp lemon juice
- 1 tbsp cornstarch
- 1 tsp vanilla extract
- 1 cup all-purpose flour
- 1 cup granulated sugar (for the topping)
- 1 1/2 tsp baking powder
- 1/4 tsp salt
- 1 cup whole milk
- 1/2 cup unsalted butter, melted

Directions

1. Set your Pit Boss to 350°F. Peach wood pellets complement the fruit's natural sweetness or applewood for a balanced, sweet smoke.
2. In a large bowl, mix the peach slices with granulated sugar, brown sugar, cinnamon, nutmeg, lemon juice, cornstarch, and vanilla extract. Stir well to coat the peaches evenly.
3. Whisk together the flour, granulated sugar, baking powder, and salt in another bowl. Add the milk and whisk until smooth. This will be your cobbler topping.
4. Pour the melted butter evenly across the bottom in a cast-iron skillet or a foil pan. Pour the batter over the melted butter, but do not stir. Spread the peach mixture evenly on top of the batter (the batter will rise up around the peaches as it cooks).
5. Place the skillet or pan in the smoker and cook for about 1 hour until the cobbler is golden brown and the peaches are bubbly. When done, the internal temperature should reach around 200°F.
6. Remove the cobbler from the smoker and let it cool for 10-15 minutes. Serve warm, preferably with a scoop of vanilla ice cream or whipped cream on top.

T I P S
- Use peach wood pellets to enhance the natural peach flavor, or try applewood for a sweet, mild smokiness.
- For different flavor profiles, swathes for other fruits like cherries, apples, or a mix of berries for a diffextural twist; sprinkle some chopped pecans or almonds over the cobbler before smoking for added crunch.

SMOKED CHEESECAKE WITH BERRY COMPOTE

Prep time: 20 min   **Cooking time: 1h 30 min**   **Serves: 8-10**

Ingredients

For the Crust
- 1 1/2 cups graham cracker crumbs
- 1/4 cup granulated sugar
- 1/2 cup unsalted butter, melted

For the Cheesecake Filling
- 24 oz cream cheese, softened
- 1 cup granulated sugar
- 3 large eggs
- 1 tsp vanilla extract
- 1/2 cup sour cream
- 1/4 cup heavy cream

For the Berry Compote
- 1 1/2 cups mixed berries (blueberries, raspberries, strawberries)
- 1/4 cup granulated sugar
- 1 tbsp lemon juice
- 1 tsp cornstarch
- 2 tbsp water

Directions

1. Set your smoker to 250°F using cherrywood or pecan pellets.
2. Mix graham cracker crumbs, sugar, and melted butter in a bowl. Press into a 9-inch springform pan to form the crust.
3. Mix softened cream cheese and sugar until smooth. Add eggs, vanilla extract, sour cream, and heavy cream.
4. Pour the cheesecake batter into the springform pan over the graham cracker crust. Smooth the top with a spatula to ensure even cooking.
5. Place the cheesecake in the smoker and cook for about 1 hour 30 minutes, or until the center is slightly jiggly but set. The internal temperature should reach 150-155°F.
6. Remove the cheesecake from the smoker and let it cool to room temperature. Once cooled, cover the cheesecake and refrigerate for at least 4 hours or overnight to fully set.
7. Combine mixed berries, sugar, and lemon juice in a saucepan. Dissolve cornstarch in water and add to the berry mixture. Cook until thickened, then let it cool.
8. Once the cheesecake is chilled, remove it from the springform pan. Serve slices topped with the berry compote.

T I P S
- Use cherrywood or pecan pellets for a subtle sweetness that complements the creamy cheesecake without overpowering it.
- For extra flavor, try adding lemon or orange zest to the cheesecake filling or mix in a swirl of berry puree before smoking.
- Place a small pan of water inside the smoker to create a humid environment, prevent cracking, and keep the cheesecake smooth and creamy.

SAUCES AND RUBS

CLASSIC BBQ SAUCE

Prep time: 10 min   Cooking time: 20 min   Serves: 8-10

Ingredients

- 1 1/2 cups ketchup
- 1/2 cup apple cider vinegar
- 1/4 cup brown sugar
- 1/4 cup molasses
- 2 tbsp Worcestershire sauce
- 1 tbsp Dijon mustard
- 1 tbsp smoked paprika
- 1 tsp garlic powder
- 1 tsp onion powder
- 1/2 tsp black pepper
- 1/4 tsp cayenne pepper (optional for heat)

Directions

1. In a medium saucepan, combine all the ingredients.
2. Bring the mixture to a simmer over medium heat, stirring occasionally.
3. Let it cook for 15-20 minutes until the sauce has thickened slightly.
4. Remove from heat and let it cool before using. Store any leftovers in an airtight container in the fridge for up to 2 weeks.

TIPS
- Best with: Pork ribs, chicken, and brisket.
- Variations: Add 2 tbsp of honey or maple syrup for a sweeter sauce. Increase the cayenne pepper or add a dash of hot sauce for extra heat.

CITRUS HERB MARINADE

Prep time: 10 min   Cooking time: 0 min   Serves: 1 cup

Ingredients

- 1/2 cup olive oil
- 1/4 cup lemon juice
- 2 tbsp orange juice
- 2 tbsp fresh thyme, chopped
- 1 tbsp fresh rosemary, chopped
- 1 tbsp garlic, minced
- 1 tsp lemon zest
- Salt and pepper to taste

Directions

1. Whisk together the olive oil, lemon juice, orange juice, thyme, rosemary, garlic, and lemon zest in a small bowl.
2. Season with salt and pepper to taste.
3. Use immediately or refrigerate for up to 3 days.

TIPS
- Best with: Chicken, pork chops, or seafood like shrimp or salmon.
- Variations: Add a dash of soy sauce or Dijon mustard for extra depth of flavor.

HONEY MUSTARD GLAZE

Prep time: 5 min   **Cooking time: 0 min**   **Serves: 6-8**

Ingredients

- 1/2 cup Dijon mustard
- 1/4 cup honey
- 1 tbsp apple cider vinegar
- 1 tsp garlic powder
- 1/2 tsp paprika
- Salt and pepper to taste

Directions

1. Whisk together the Dijon mustard, honey, vinegar, garlic powder, and paprika in a small bowl.
2. Season with salt and pepper to taste.
3. Use immediately as a glaze for meats or refrigerate for up to 1 week.

TIPS

- Best with: Chicken, pork, or roasted vegetables like carrots and Brussels sprouts.
- Variations: Add a touch of heat with 1/4 tsp cayenne or a dash of hot sauce.

COFFEE SPICE RUB

Prep time: 5 min   **Cooking time: 0 min**   **Serves: 1 cup**

Ingredients

- 1/4 cup ground coffee (freshly ground)
- 2 tbsp brown sugar
- 1 tbsp smoked paprika
- 1 tbsp kosher salt
- 1 tbsp black pepper
- 1 tsp ground cumin
- 1 tsp garlic powder
- 1 tsp onion powder
- 1/2 tsp cayenne pepper (optional)

Directions

1. Combine all ingredients in a small bowl and mix well.
2. Store in an airtight container for up to 3 months.
3. Use liberally on steaks, ribs, or brisket before grilling or smoking.

TIPS

- Best with: Beef steaks, brisket, and pork ribs.
- Variations: Use espresso powder instead of ground coffee for a more intense coffee flavor.

MAPLE BOURBON GLAZE

Ingredients

- 1/2 cup maple syrup
- 1/4 cup bourbon
- 2 tbsp Dijon mustard
- 1 tbsp soy sauce
- 1 tbsp brown sugar
- 1 garlic clove, minced
- 1/2 tsp black pepper

Directions

1. Combine the maple syrup, bourbon, Dijon mustard, soy sauce, brown sugar, garlic, and black pepper in a small saucepan.
2. Bring to a simmer over medium heat, stirring occasionally. Let cook for 10-15 minutes, until the sauce has thickened slightly.
3. Remove from heat and let cool before using.

TIPS
- Best with: Pork chops, salmon, or roasted vegetables.
- Variations: Add 1 tsp of smoked paprika for a smoky depth or 1 tbsp of apple cider vinegar for extra tang.

TANGY CAROLINA MUSTARD SAUCE

Ingredients

- 1 cup yellow mustard
- 1/4 cup apple cider vinegar
- 1/4 cup honey
- 2 tbsp brown sugar
- 1 tbsp Worcestershire sauce
- 1 tsp garlic powder
- 1 tsp onion powder
- 1/2 tsp cayenne pepper (optional for heat)
- Salt and black pepper to taste

Directions

1. In a medium saucepan, whisk together the mustard, apple cider vinegar, honey, brown sugar, Worcestershire sauce, garlic powder, onion powder, and cayenne pepper (if using).
2. Place the saucepan over medium heat and bring the mixture to a simmer.
3. Cook for about 8-10 minutes, stirring occasionally, until the sauce thickens slightly.
4. Remove from heat and let the sauce cool to room temperature.
5. Adjust seasoning with salt and pepper to taste.
6. Store in an airtight container in the refrigerator for up to 2 weeks.

TIPS
- Best with: Pulled pork, smoked chicken, or sausages.
- Variations: Add a splash of hot sauce for extra spice or a tablespoon of ketchup to balance the tanginess with a hint of sweetness.

ASIAN-INSPIRED MARINADE

Prep time: 10 min **Cooking time: 0 min** **Serves: 1 cup**

Ingredients

- 1/4 cup soy sauce
- 1/4 cup rice vinegar
- 2 tbsp sesame oil
- 1 tbsp honey
- 1 tbsp fresh ginger, grated
- 1 garlic clove, minced
- 1 tbsp sesame seeds (optional)

Directions

1. Whisk together the soy sauce, rice vinegar, sesame oil, honey, ginger, and garlic in a small bowl.
2. Stir in sesame seeds if using.
3. Use immediately or store in the refrigerator for up to 3 days.

TIPS

- Best with: Beef, chicken, or tofu.
- Variations: Add a touch of heat with a dash of sriracha or red pepper flakes.

MEDITERRANEAN DRY RUB

Prep time: 5 min **Cooking time: 0 min** **Serves: 1/2 cup**

Ingredients

- 2 tbsp dried oregano
- 2 tbsp dried thyme
- 1 tbsp ground cumin
- 1 tbsp paprika
- 2 tsp garlic powder
- 1 tsp black pepper
- 1 tsp kosher salt

Directions

1. Combine all ingredients in a small bowl and mix well.
2. Store in an airtight container for up to 6 months.
3. Rub generously over lamb, chicken, or vegetables before grilling.

TIPS

- Best with: Lamb, chicken, or eggplant.
- Variations: Add 1 tsp ground coriander for a brighter, citrus-like flavor.

CHIMICHURRI SAUCE

Prep time: 10 min   Cooking time: 0 min   Serves: 6-8

Ingredients

- 1/2 cup fresh parsley, chopped
- 1/4 cup fresh cilantro, chopped
- 1/4 cup red wine vinegar
- 1/4 cup olive oil
- 4 garlic cloves, minced
- 1 tsp red pepper flakes (optional)
- Salt and pepper to taste

Directions

1. Mix the parsley, cilantro, garlic, red wine vinegar, and olive oil in a small bowl.
2. Stir in the red pepper flakes, and season with salt and pepper to taste.
3. Let sit for at least 15 minutes to allow flavors to meld before serving.

TIPS

- Best with: Grilled steak, chicken, or shrimp.
- Variations: Add a splash of lime juice for a tangy twist, or substitute mint for a refreshing flavor.

SMOKY CINNAMON RUB

Prep time: 5 min   Cooking time: 0 min   Serves: 1/2 cup

Ingredients

- 2 tbsp smoked paprika
- 1 tbsp cinnamon
- 1 tbsp brown sugar
- 1 tbsp kosher salt
- 1 tsp black pepper
- 1 tsp ground cumin
- 1/2 tsp cayenne pepper (optional)

Directions

1. Combine all ingredients in a small bowl and mix well.
2. Store in an airtight container for up to 6 months.
3. Use generously on pork, chicken, or vegetables before smoking or grilling.

TIPS

- Best with: Pork, sweet potatoes, and roasted squash.
- Variations: Add 1 tsp ground cloves or nutmeg for a warmer, more complex flavor.

FINAL REFLECTIONS ON MASTERY OF THE GRILL

CONCLUSIONS

As we wrap up this guide on making the most of your Pit Boss Wood Pellet Grill, let's take a moment to reflect on the path we've walked together. From familiarizing yourself with your grill to mastering the ins and outs of direct and indirect grilling, diving into the art of smoking, and playing with different pellet flavors, you've gained knowledge to elevate your grilling game and expand your barbecue skills.

We started by focusing on the essentials—getting to know your Pit Boss's unique features and understanding why wood pellet grilling stands out. We also touched on the key safety practices to remember, ensuring every grilling session is enjoyable and safe. From there, we explored your grill's versatility, looking at how direct grilling brings a perfect sear to steaks and burgers. In contrast, indirect grilling allows for slow cooking and even roasting, which is ideal for larger cuts of meat or delicate dishes.

As we ventured further, we uncovered the potential of your Pit Boss to be more than just a grill. Whether smoking a brisket, roasting a chicken, or even baking a pizza, the Pit Boss is an all-in-one outdoor cooking companion. The role of wood pellets also came into focus —how each variety can subtly or boldly influence the flavor of your food, from hickory's robust smokiness to the milder, sweeter notes of applewood. Knowing how to mix and match these pellets allows you to customize each meal to suit your taste and creativity.

Now that you're armed with these insights and tips it's important to remember that mastering your Pit Boss is about more than just following techniques—it's about embracing the process. Every grilling session is an opportunity to sharpen your skills, try new recipes, and discover the perfect balance of heat, smoke, and flavor. With each successful cook, your confidence grows, and so does your enthusiasm to keep pushing the limits of what you can create.

But grilling isn't just about food; it's about the whole experience—the joy of being outside, the satisfaction of working with your hands, and the excitement of serving up something that brings people together. Your Pit Boss isn't just a tool; it's a gateway to creating memories with friends and family, building connections over shared meals, and enjoying the simple pleasure of a perfectly grilled dish. The camaraderie that grilling fosters is hard to match, and that sense of community makes outdoor cooking unique.

As this guide draws closer, remember that even the best grill masters started as beginners. Each time you fire up your Pit Boss, you learn, experiment, and improve. Whether tackling a new cut of meat or fine-tuning a familiar recipe, every cookout brings you one step closer to mastering the craft. Embrace the challenges, celebrate the victories, and explore the vast, flavorful world of wood pellet grilling.

This journey doesn't end here. There's always a new recipe, a new pellet combination to test, and a new way to surprise your taste buds. With your Pit Boss, the possibilities are endless, and every grilling session is a chance to grow, learn, and—most importantly—enjoy the ride. So light up those pellets, and get ready to impress with your next barbecue masterpiece!

SCAN THE QR CODE
AND
GET YOUR BONUSES NOW!

Or copy and paste the following link:

https://pietrofiore.aweb.page/p/10e0982f-7136-4b4f-8d45-2513ebcb97a3

Made in the USA
Coppell, TX
21 December 2024

43336522R00046